DEVIATING VOI

Suffolk County Council

Women and orthodox
religious tradition

BU 3M

DEVIATING VOICES

Women and orthodox religious tradition

S.W. Jackman

The Lutterworth Press
Cambridge

The Lutterworth Press
P.O. Box 60
Cambridge
CB1 2NT

www.lutterworth.com
publishing@lutterworth.com

ISBN 0 7188 3024 5

British Library Cataloguing in Publication Data
A catalogue record is available from the British Library

Copyright © S.W. Jackman, 2003

First Published in 2003

All rights reserved. No part of this edition may be reproduced,
stored in a retrieval system, or transmitted in any form or by any means,
electronic mechanical, photocopying, recording or otherwise, without the
prior permission in writing from the Publisher.

Printed in the United Kingdom by
MFP Print

Contents

Introduction	7
1. Elizabeth Barton	11
2. Teresa Sanchez de Cepeda y Ahumad	25
3. Jeanne Marie Guyon	37
4. Selina, Countess of Huntingdon	47
5. Anne Lee	61
6. Joanna Southcott	71
7. Barbara Juliana, Baroness de Krudener	81
8. Elizabeth Sellon	97
9. Mary Baker Eddy	107
10. Helena Petrvna Blavatsky	125
11. Ethel Cecilia Dodd	143
12. Aimée Semple Macpherson	159
Bibliography	172
Index	174

Illustrations

A hanging at Tyburn	10
Bernini's statue of St Teresa	24
Madam Guyon	36
Selina, Countess of Hastings	46
Ann Lee's Tomb	60
Joanna Southcott	70
Baroness de Krudener and her daughter (Angelika Kauffmann)	80
Lydia Sellon	96
Mary Baker Eddy	110
Madam Blavatsky	114
Cecilia Dodd and friend	142
Aimée Semple Macpherson	158

Introduction

The writings of St Paul with respect to the role of women in religious life are well known: he would have them keep their silence and their heads covered. St John Chrysostom held women in low regard referring to them as "merely a whitened sepulchre". His contemporary, St Augustine, observed, "By the sex of her body she, woman kind, is submissive to the masculine sex." Things did not improve over the centuries with the verse, "For we courtiers learn at school, only with our sex to fool. Y're not worth the serious part." "The Great Cham" himself, Doctor Johnson, remarked, "Sir, a woman preaching is like a dog walking on his hinder legs. It is not done well, but you are surprised to see it done at all." The nineteenth-century Tractarian clergyman, Edward Pusey, stated that "The female character expands but in the shade." In the Anglican Church of today there are a number of adherents who object to the ordination of women as priests, and very much so to episcopal office. In both the Roman Catholic and Orthodox communions the idea of women in anything but a very limited role is totally rejected by officialdom.

Despite these animadversions, there were deviating voices from the earliest days of the Christian church. Maximilla, a Montanist, having personally received the Holy Spirit was to prophesy disasters following her demise, saying, "After me there will be no further prophets, only the end". By "the end" she meant the immediate Second Coming. Priscilla, whose religious views were not dissimilar, was also a prophetess who "spoke in tongues", glossolalia, and was a convinced millenarian. These Montanist views were condemned by the orthodox, and their adherents branded as heretics. The mediaeval church had those, who in one way or another, challenged the assumptions of St Paul; these women were not rebels, but rather re-inventing the female role. Saints such as Bridget of Sweden and Catherine of Siena had a real influence on church life. Later St Teresa of Avila must have been a great trial to her ecclesiastical supervisions as she junketed about Spain with her entourage and dragged poor St John of the Cross in her wake as she established various Discalced Carmelite communities.

Two sixteenth-century English women, Anne Askew and Joan Boucher, were dissidents. The former held decidedly heretical views on the sacrament, and asserted them publicly. She was to be burned at the stake in 1546. Her contemporary, Joan Boucher, distributed copies of Tyndale's translation of the New Testament, rejected by the orthodox, to ladies of the court. She, too, was burned at the stake in 1550 for holding what were essentially docetic opinions.

Antoinette Bourignon founded an orphanage in the mid-seventeenth century, where the children were taught to believe they were truly "imps of Satan" being possessed by devils. She preached a curious mélange of Jansenist and Pelagian ideas, which made her unpopular with both Protestants and Catholics in her native Belgium. Her French near-contemporary, Angélique Arnaud, who was also French, and a notorious Jansenist, had grave reservations about the virtues attributed to the masculine sex – in particular with respect to monks and priests. She did not hesitate in making these opinions known. Her views on royal personages were equally unflattering. She said, for example, of princesses that few could be found in which the spirit and grace of God were evident. It is hardly surprising that King Louis XIV found this descendant of a Cathar family not to his liking.

Anne Hutchinson fell foul of the authorities in the Massachusetts Bay Colony in 1637 for advocating antinomianism, and was expelled to Rhode Island. Her enemies rightly felt that she had received her just desserts when she was killed by Indians a few years later. Another North American, Jemima Wilkinson, claimed to have died in 1776, and returned with a new body as an incarnation of Christ. She dressed in semi-masculine costume, and asserted her ability to perform miracles. She claimed to emulate Christ in being able to walk on water, her followers seem to have believed this implicitly but she appears never to have been put to the test.

While in general John Wesley did not favour women preachers, it seems that on occasion his sister Patty Wesley and also Sarah Crosly did deliver the occasional sermon. On the other hand, William Booth, the founder of the Salvation Army, encouraged his wife, Catherine Booth, to preach the gospel. Indeed, a Salvation Army placard advertised her activities with the words, "Come and hear a woman preach!"

More eccentric perhaps were the Fox sisters who were spiritualists, and who claimed to be able to communicate with the dead. Traditional Christian denominations were hostile to such assertions. Annie Besant, one-time atheist and later a leading figure in the Theosophical Society, was to promote Jiddu Krishnamurti as almost a semi-divine world teacher. Perhaps equally curious was the career of Alexandra David Neel, a some-time French opera singer, who travelled to India, visited Tibet and wrote on Tibetan Buddhism. She was in later life to establish a centre in France which became a sort of lamasary.

It is obvious, therefore, that deviating voices, one might almost say dissenting voices, are infinitely varied. The women critics who, for example, remained members of the Roman Catholic Church were not silenced by traditional authority. They were essentially reformers not revolutionaries, but rejected the orthodoxy of the world of which they were a part, and they were prepared to risk persecution, and in some instances death to advance their opinions. There were those also who were convinced it was their destiny to lead society to a better set of beliefs that would ensure their earthly happiness and their ultimate salvation. All of them, one way and another, had a vision, some literally, others only in the generic sense of the word. To succeed they could have no doubts as to the rightness of their mission. It is obvious that had they been men their ideas might well have found more support and their activities greater approbation. Religious life has since the start of the Christian era been dominated by men, who made the rules and determined what was acceptable. They often regarded women who might in some fashion challenge the establishment with very real hostility.

One deviating voice, that of the unworldly Joanna Southcott, might well symbolise what all of these women were attempted to accomplish. She said, "This is a New thing Amongst mankind for a woman to be the Greatest Prophet that ever came into the world, to bring man out of darkness into thy Marvellous light and make every Crooked path straight before You, and bring every mountain to a plain, and all dark sayings shall be brought into Light."

Elizabeth Barton

If the road to hell be paved with good intentions surely the ghastly fate that ultimately befell Elizabeth Barton is proof enough of such an aphorism. Certainly, on the best of interpretations of her life, one cannot accuse her of pure malice, but foolishness, indiscretion and lack of political awareness very definitely. She lived in a harsh age, and consorted with individuals often more sophisticated than herself whose motives were not as pure as her own.

Elizabeth Barton, known as the Nun of Canterbury or alternatively as the Holy Maid of Kent, was born in 1506. Her place of birth is not precisely known – there is some evidence that it was in the village of Aldington – and her family history remains obscure. Her only recorded relation was a sister, but her ultimate history is lost. From about the age of nineteen she was employed in the household of Thomas Cobb. The latter was the steward of an estate possibly belonging to Archbishop Warham who also owned the manor of Aldington.

The parish of Aldington seemed to have been a desirable living, having been held by Thomas Linacre, physician, scholar and preceptor of Henry VIII's elder daughter, the Princess Mary. During much of Elizabeth Barton's life the cure was held by Richard Masters who apparently coped with the vagaries of the religious establishment residing comfortably through all the changes until 1569.

The role played by Richard Masters in Elizabeth Barton's early career is unclear. It was presumed that his sermons inspired her later visions, and that he may have taught her certain verses of scripture to assist in her devotions. Certainly, however, he was never a party to any sort of fraudulent or false prophecies later attributed to her. The same cannot be said so precisely about Edward Bocking who was to be closely associated with her in Canterbury.

From the extant evidence of her earlier medical history it would seem that she suffered from epilepsy. Her health was at no time particularly good, but such was the regard in which she appears to have been held by the Cobb family she continued as a dependant. In 1525 she went into a sort of coma, and for some days was unconscious and in much mental distress. While in this state she seems to have foretold the death of a child of Thomas Cobb being very precise as to the day and the time. Naturally, such an utterance with its consequences created a very considerable impression on the village.

The initial trance was to be followed by others in increasing frequency. When in such a state her face was, according to local reports, contorted, her throat showed obvious swellings, and she lay rigid and immobile. While in this condition her remarks were divisible into two categories. In one she may be said to be clairvoyant, describing events and activities which occurred elsewhere and of which, under ordinary circumstances, she could have no possible knowledge. Her speech, while making these pronouncements, was precise and clear. Her other sort of commentaries were of a theological nature. She talked in a coherent manner of heaven, purgatory and hell in a highly orthodox fashion, and these remarks were in no way heretical. It was observed that when she spoke of heaven and good things her voice was sweet and melodious while, on the contrary, when observing of the pains of hell and purgatory her voice acquired an almost demonic tone and could quite terrify her hearers. It was reported, too, that she uttered much of her remarks without seeming to move her lips, which of course added to the peculiarity of her situation.

While in a trance she seems to have directed her audience to attend mass on a regular basis, admonished her fellow villagers to make special prayers to the Virgin against the dangers of Satan, and promoted the Christian life generally. She appears also to have had visions and was something of a clairvoyant. She insisted that society must repudiate the corruptions of the world, and advocated the traditional values of the Church. At times she also seems to have given highly sophisticated expositions on abstruse theological matters. Critics and enemies later were to imply that on these occasions she was being coached by Masters and later by Edward Bocking.

To accuse Masters of devious behaviour is highly unfair. He seems to have been sincerely impressed by his parishioner. Moreover, his actions regarding her were most sensible. He was an intelligent and educated man, and decided to act in a realistic fashion concerning the various prophetic sayings of Elizabeth Barton. He wrote a lengthy letter to Archbishop Warham describing the state of affairs in his parish. The Archbishop ordered that an investigation be made and two Benedictine monks and two Friars Observants were to join Richard Masters to resolve the matter.

The commission put a number of queries to Elizabeth Barton, and they found no reason to doubt her orthodoxy and no evidence of heresy or demonic possession. To celebrate the favourable report she and a considerable group of adherents went to a chapel at Court-at-Street. In this chapel it was noted that previously she had fallen into a coma, and it was said that she had remained in such a state for nine days taking neither food nor drink. On this second occasion she again went into a trance-like state, and from the contemporary evidence her face became contorted, her tongue extended, her eyes protruded; it would seem to be an epileptic fit. She spoke of the Virgin, the importance of total adherence to the Christian faith, anathematised all the opponents of the Catholic Church, and of the certainty that such heretics were doomed to damnation. At this time she also avowed that God had directed her to accept Edward Bocking as her spiritual advisor, and that she was to become a nun. On emerging from her trance she appears, as have other mystics, to have had no recollection of her statements. These events were to be recorded in a tract entitled, *A Miraculous work of Late done at Court-at-Street in Kent, published to the Devout People of the Tyme for their Spiritual Consolation*. It appeared in 1527 and was written by Edward Thwaites.

With the report of the commission, and the account of the events at Court-at-Street, Archbishop Warham apparently accepted the facts as presented. However, he was a notoriously cautious individual and sent a copy to be placed before the King. The latter appears to have perused the contents in a casual fashion and, after reading, gave it to Thomas More, who, like his sovereign, evidently found nothing heretical or politically dangerous in Warham's communication, and the whole affair was thought to be of little consequence. Other women had similar experiences and, indeed, More had openly supported the supposed divine inspirations of Anne Wentworth, "the Maid of Ipswich", whose prophesying was not dissimilar to that of Elizabeth Barton.

Following her experiences at Court-at-Street her general health was much improved, and it was thought that her recovery was due to the miraculous intervention of the Virgin. Those who had previously expressed doubts were now totally certain that she was a holy individual.

The Church authorities decided that she should enter the Benedictine convent at St Sepulchre in Canterbury. Initially, the prioress was somewhat reluctant to accept the new postulant: her general ill health, despite the seemingly miraculous cure, and her lack of a dowry were put forward as objections. St Sepulchre was a small and impoverished institution but through Bocking it was avowed that the Virgin had decreed that all would be well. Having a visionary as a member of the community could bring its own problems. The prioress allowed herself to be convinced, and as Elizabeth Barton was a protégé of the Archbishop, permitted her to join the small community of five professed nuns and herself. It was at this time that Elizabeth Barton becomes more widely known as "The Nun of Kent".

For the next couple of years her prophetic powers and theological preaching continued. The subject matter was varied. On occasion she asserted that although physically in Canterbury, her spiritual body was transported to the little chapel at Court-at-Street. The chapel had been much improved owing to its association with Elizabeth Barton, and was often visited by the pious. She was now no longer the serving maid of Thomas Cobb but the Reverend Dame Elizabeth Barton, O.S.B. Incidentally, the fact that she could become a fully professed choir nun indicated that probably she was fully literate being able to read and write in Latin. On occasion Warham would despatch collections of her oracular pronouncements to London, but the King seems to have been completely indifferent to their import or significance.

Up to this point her ecstatic exhortations brought her only notoriety. It was said that "Divers and many as well as great men of the realm and mean men and many learned men but especially religious men had great confidence in her and often resorted to her". Her supporters regarded her utterances as being divinely inspired, and she had few detractors. She was, however, to be attacked by Tyndale in 1530 as an impostor; she with Anne Wentworth were to him "false, dissembling harlots". His criticisms would have had little consequence but for the advent of "The King's Great Matter".

In 1528, King Henry VIII began to discuss with his advisors, and in particular with the Archbishop of York, Cardinal Wolsey, who was the King's chief minister, his doubts about the validity of his marriage to Catherine of Aragon, his brother's widow. A dispensation from the Pope had been given to allow the nuptials which otherwise would have been regarded as contrary to divine and canon law. Henry avowed that in entering such a marriage he and Catherine had sinned, and that the sign of God's displeasure was that they had no living male offspring. The heir to the throne was their daughter, Mary, born in 1516. English history really had no real precedent for a Queen regnant. While Henry I's daughter, the Empress Maud, ruled in her own right during the civil war of 1141-1147, the anarchy of those years was probably a major reason for the prejudice against regnant queens.

The King, perhaps naively, believed that a divorce could be obtained through Wolsey's influence in Rome but political events on the continent made it impossible, as the Pope was the virtual prisoner of Catherine of Aragon's nephew, the Emperor Charles V, and was therefore disinclined to do anything that might make his situation worse. At this juncture Elizabeth Barton was only marginally involved, merely stating that disaster would ensue if princes failed in their obedience to the church.

In the autumn of 1528, Archbishop Warham wrote a letter to his colleague, Wolsey, to introduce Elizabeth Barton to him. She had proposed that she should have an audience with the King and also with Wolsey. Warham, cautious as always, indicated that she was pious and virtuous.

Upon reaching London, she was granted an audience with Wolsey. She informed him that she was inspired by the Archangel Michael to say that if he or Warham furthered the King's divorce, and proposed marriage to Anne Boleyn they would be utterly destroyed. When Wolsey heard these remarks apparently he became alarmed. From her comments, it would seem that he would court damnation if he supported the monarch and risk death if he objected. He temporised, and arranged that she should confront the King directly.

Elizabeth Barton apparently had no qualms about the consequences of her utterances. In the royal presence she said that she had been instructed by the Archangel to say that the sovereign must not assume the rights of the papacy, that he must destroy all heretics, and that above all he must not put his proper wife from him to marry Anne Boleyn, and that if he persisted in this folly God would punish him severely.

Curiously enough, King Henry does not appear to have been unduly angered by her remarks. He seems to have listened intently enough, but totally disregarded their import, assuming they were utterances of a deranged person being convinced of the rightness of his cause. Elizabeth Barton was sent back to Canterbury.

The visit to London was to be the first of several. She again visited Wolsey, and on each occasion she reiterated her previous remarks prophesying his fall from grace and power and his ignominious fate because of his failure to obey the will of God. She seems also to have had another royal audience with the King in December 1529 at Haworth observing that the Angel said that he, the King, was acting against God's will and that if he persisted he would not long remain the sovereign, "he should not be King thereof one day, not one hour after [presumably following his marriage to Anne Boleyn]" and that "he should die a shameful and miserable death". It would seem that in her confrontation with the King it was in a humble fashion kneeling before him and with tears beseeched him not to divorce Queen Catherine for the good of his soul and for the welfare of the country. Again Henry seems to have been moderate in his reaction to what she said. He was, it appears, impressed by her sincerity and by her obvious piety. Apparently, he tried to persuade her of the rightness of his cause, but without success. Once again she was required to return to Canterbury.

On the way home she proceeded first to Rochester where she met Bishop John Fisher. Apparently, she told him all that she had said to the King and what had been the sovereign's reaction. Fisher evidently was much perturbed however when she indicated that the monarch was adamant in pursuing his course of action.

Although consorting with the mighty, she did not abandon her faithful adherents. Upon reaching Canterbury she had another vision, rather more mundane. Several young monks had contemplated joining Tyndale in Antwerp. The Angel, she avowed, would ensure that the weather would be so inclement that the boat could not depart. Hence, the souls of these youthful dissidents were saved. The Angel also said that any person who was so misguided as to have a copy of Tyndale's bible should burn it immediately otherwise they would risk damnation.

Meanwhile Wolsey's career had come to an end because he had been unable to procure Henry's divorce. His death, too, was, as she had predicted, a solitary and melancholy event. However, she asserted that he was not totally damned, the devil wanted his soul, but he was allowed to remain in limbo until a final judgement ensued. She prayed for his deliverance, he was released and passed into heaven by her efforts. Wolsey was certainly no saint, and she was well aware of the fact but he had not succumbed to the temptation of earthly vanity and acceded to the King's wishes, he had not granted the sovereign a divorce and hence was not all evil. Other counsellors such as Stephen Gardiner, Edmund Bonner and Cuthbert Tunstall, all clerics, were not so virtuous.

She was now venturing into more dangerous waters. She continued to admonish and chastise the ungodly. She preached against Luther and the reformers. She insisted that all Christians must accept papal authority unquestioning. She claimed she had seen purgatory and hell and knew the torments that awaited the ungodly. She did not regard herself as a perfect being. She often lusted and desired sexual pleasure, as she said to her confessor Edward Bocking. She claimed the devil had attempted to seduce her and to have her perform sexual acts with him and to indulge in lewd behaviour. To save herself she had called upon her protectors the angels, in particular the Archangel Michael, to rescue her. Indeed, modern psychologists would declare that many of her visions were typical hallucinatory experiences.

She also counselled others who had mystical visions. One such individual was Elizabeth of Tottenham. Elizabeth Barton, perhaps seeing her as a potential rival, decided that Elizabeth of Tottenham's visions were inspired by Satan, and warned her against them. She seems to have been successful in her endeavours because Elizabeth of Tottenham ceased to have ecstatic experiences. Her success in this instance was reported to Thomas More who concluded that she was a pious and holy person.

Her prophetic utterances continued in an antigovernment mode. She declared that no person should attempt to deprive Princess Mary of her rank and position, a reference to the possible legislation declaring her a bastard. Moreover, if the Emperor Charles V came to Mary's assistance all good Christians should rally to her side. By now she was very hostile to the King and his adherents, and her position was not dissimilar to that of most conservatives both lay and clerical. Her many sayings had considerable circulation, and were published in a number of tracts. A direct confrontation with royal authority was inevitable.

Further, she turned her attention to Archbishop Warham whom she saw as a weak person. She predicted what would happen at his death if he persisted in supporting the crown. She was convinced that her warnings of his dire fate, and ultimate damnation, made him an opponent of the King. Indeed, Thomas Cranmer, Warham's successor, was to assert that she exerted very real influence over both Wolsey and Warham. When the latter died in 1532, because he, too, had not surrendered to royal despotism, his soul was saved and ascended into heaven accompanied by St Thomas. Without her advocacy she was certain he would have capitulated and consequently been damned.

Warham personally had always been a moderating influence on her pronouncements, and with his death she became less and less rational. She was more radical in her public statements and predictions being totally unwilling or unaware to see potential dangers. More confirmed opponents of royal policy were now public allies, and she was championed by such reactionaries as Henry Gold who wrote to his fellow clerics pressing her virtues.

The nuns at Syon were to become involved with her public utterances. These nuns were particularly important because of their associations with the Courtenays and the Poles, who had connections with the previous dynasty, the house of York. She openly supported the pretensions of the Marquess of Exeter to the throne despite her championing of Princess Mary. In due course her activities were to bring both Exeter and Montague to the block. She uttered dire threats as to what might befall the papal agents, Silvestre Davio and Antonio Pollio, unless they actively supported Queen Catherine and Princess Mary. She even predicted a terrible future for Pope Clement VII if he failed to support the injured queen and her daughter. So powerful did she seem to be that the friends and relations of Anne Boleyn sought to bribe her to be silent, but without success. She went so far as to declare that she had been instrumental in preventing a marriage between the King and Anne Boleyn at Calais.

When the royal couple returned to England they visited Canterbury. She forced herself into their company, repeated her admonitions against the proposed nuptials, and predicted that if they did occur the King would shortly die following the loss of his throne. Again, she said that his policies would bring grief and distress to the kingdom with plagues and destruction. Soon after this event she went to the chapel at Court-at-Street, and before the statue of the Virgin she declared that Queen Catherine would prosper and that Princess Mary would one day be queen. She tried hard to gain an audience with Queen Catherine but failed. Neither Catherine nor her daughter was prepared to risk their fate by associating with the radical nun.

Inevitably, the question arises as to what degree she was manipulated by those individuals directly or indirectly in opposition to King Henry VIII. It is evident that the Yorkist faction still had ambitions to regain the crown, and were not above some quiet plotting. Their activities were not unknown to Thomas Cromwell, Wolsey's successor as chief minister, by means of informers.

One of her most prominent supporters was Hugh Rich, a well-known preacher. He had extolled Elizabeth Barton to Bishop Fisher. He also reported on her supposed vision with respect to St Mary Magdalene. This particularly interested Fisher who was involved with the vexatious question of how many St Mary Magdalenes there were. Some authorities asserted there were three. When Bishop Fisher put the question to Elizabeth Barton she asserted there was only one. This confirmed Fisher's own view and reaffirmed the assumption he had made in a book that he had written over a decade previously.

Rich also conversed with More on the subject of the Nun of Kent. More sensibly declined to consider seriously anything she had said with respect to the King.

She was still at liberty to see people and to make oracular statements. She received Silvestre Davio, the papal nuncio to Scotland, on his return to Rome. She repeated her prediction to him that the King would soon die if he married Anne Boleyn. She was evidently totally unaware that the couple had been secretly married for some months. She told Davio that if Pope Clement acceded to the royal divorce he would suffer various painful afflictions. Moreover, he was to use his position to blacken King Henry's reputation as frequently as possible. On a visit to Syon Abbey she told Lady Exeter her husband would inherit the crown; this despite the fact that earlier she had asserted that Princess Mary would become queen with Lord Montague, another Yorkist, as her consort. All of these tergiversations on the part of Elizabeth Barton and her friends made the royal advisors highly suspicious. As yet there was no overt treason, but proposing or wishing the death of the sovereign was a matter of serious concern and this could lead either to the scaffold or to Tyburn.

In the summer of 1533 Thomas More finally acted. He wrote a letter to her saying that she should not cause people to believe things that probably would not happen. He reminded her of the folly of Nicholas Hopkins, who had so encouraged the Duke of Buckingham in his pretensions that finally ruined him. In other words, he indicated that Elizabeth Barton could destroy the Courtenay family and all of the Yorkist connections.

She had asserted that the Angel had told her that if the King married Anne Boleyn he would lose his throne within a month. This did not occur; he continued to hold the crown without any adverse effects. One is tempted to wonder why people remained so credulous and continued to believe her prognostications. Her supporters took the position that the monarch had no real right to the throne, having lost divine approbation. Such assertions cannot but have perturbed and irritated men like Cromwell because what she was implying was that an insurrection, should it occur, would have not only papal and imperial but also divine approbation.

The monastic communities seem to have been particularly enthusiastic about her revelations, not only in Canterbury but elsewhere, such as at Sheen. The monks promoted her revelations in various communications among themselves, and this propaganda ensured that she was being taken seriously.

In the summer of 1533 the royal authorities determined to act, and Cromwell arranged for Cranmer to conduct an interrogation as to whether she was sincere and honest. The meeting took place on 23 July at Sevenoaks, where Cranmer was then residing. Despite the many rumours about her and her associates she was apparently, at this juncture, deemed to be not particularly dangerous. She was released and allowed to make a further pilgrimage to Court-at-Street, where her career as a mystic had begun. More surprisingly, perhaps, she was permitted to be there on 15 August, the Feast of the Virgin's Assumption, for her and her adherents a very special day of holy obligation.

Her liberty was not to be of long standing. She was, a few weeks later, placed under a form of house arrest, and was interviewed by Cranmer, Cromwell and Hugh Latimer, the Bishop of Worcester. At this juncture she declared, "She never had visions in all her life, but all that she ever said was feigned of her own imagination, only to satisfy the minds of those which resorted to her, and to obtain worldly praise." Privately she may have warned her close friends that her volte-face was a lie, and that it was for her own defence and their protection. She appears to have also told them that her revelations were in fact true and divinely inspired as they had believed.

The commission ordered the arrest of Edward Bocking and Thomas Hadleigh. Bocking was thought to have been the principal person involved in her imposture. Soon other of her associates, Richard Masters, the parish priest of Aldington, Hugh Rich and Richard Roley, Friars Observant, Richard Deving, Henry Gold, Thomas Gold and Henry Thwaites, were imprisoned. While under arrest she gave an example of her so-called ecstasy. She told the commission that certain priests gave her information from the confessional which she was able to use to ensure her knowledge had a divine source. She also said that the nuncio had told her that the pope intended to preach a crusade against the king, and that he would be deposed and die in exile. She was to say in the presence of her friends Edward Bocking and Henry and Thomas Gold that all her revelations were mere inventions. The poor deluded men then said to her, "Woe be the time that ever thee were born for thine ungraciousness and false dissembling hath undone us all." They declared her to have been the falsest creature that ever lived for having deceived them so cruelly. All three men threw themselves on the mercy of the court.

The next step was a sort of trial. King Henry summoned an assembly of notables to determine the fate of Elizabeth Barton and her close associates. They debated for three days; on the last of them the accused were present. The Lord Chancellor, Sir Thomas Audley, declared that she and the other accused had plotted rebellion and the King's dethronement. If the crown had hoped to find evidence that Queen Catherine had been involved they were unsuccessful. Nothing existed to show that there had ever been a direct contact.

In mid-November 1533, on order of the Star Chamber, Elizabeth Barton and her nine confederates stood on a scaffold erected in front of St Paul's Cathedral, and listened to a lengthy sermon preached by the Bishop of Bangor outlining the various charges, telling the story of her life and how by the work of Bocking and the others she had gained her reputations. After an hour the sermon ended, the accused read their confessions, asserted they were deeply sorry for their actions, and, then when they were done, hoped the king would forgive them. They were then taken back to the Tower where they had been imprisoned to await upon events.

Some of the aristocracy who had been implicated decided to throw themselves on the King's mercy. Lady Exeter grovelled before King Henry, beseeching his forgiveness. Her husband likewise asked pardon. For the moment the monarch was inclined to be merciful.

The fate of Elizabeth Barton and her confederates took some time to decide. After consideration it was felt that the simplest method of getting rid of them was by attainder. This piece of legislation dispensed with any need for a proper trial. Before this was done the prisoners were returned to Canterbury where they went through the same ceremony as had taken place in London. Even the sermon was identical, although the preacher was different. The commissioners had also managed to get some 500 copies of Bocking's book praising the Maid of Kent's revelations. These copies were all ordered to be destroyed.

The government were still certain that there were other malefactors. Two in particular caught their attention, namely, Thomas More and John Fisher. More skilfully refuted all of the charges and he even reminded Cromwell that he, More, had been consulted by the king himself in 1526 with respect to Elizabeth Barton. He also asserted that, while others had tried to persuade him of the truths of Elizabeth Barton's revelations, he had always declined to support her cause. Cromwell produced evidence that she had attempted to visit More, but the latter was able to prove that such had not occurred. Cromwell begrudgingly accepted More's refutation. Less fortunate was John Fisher. He had participated more directly in the activities of the accused. He had seen her on various occasions, his apologia was less convincing than More's though he had done nothing that was actually treasonable.

The Bill of Attainder initially carried both their names, but More's was removed and Fisher was only charged with misprision of treason. More was penalised by losing his pension from the King while Fisher was placed under house arrest. The bill became law on 24 March 1534 having receiving royal assent some fifteen minutes after parliament was prorogued.

Some three weeks later Elizabeth Barton and her priestly companions were lashed to hurdles. Elizabeth Barton being the principal malefactor had a hurdle to herself. She was dressed in a shift; her companions, not garbed in priestly dress, wore cast-off gowns. It took two hours to get from the Tower to Tyburn.

Elizabeth Barton was the first to be executed. It seems she made a brief speech, repeated her confession, that she was responsible for her own death and that of her companions. She begged the populace to pray for her soul. She was hanged and left for dead, being only cut down when life was extinct. The corpse was then beheaded and the trunk buried in the cemetery of the Grey Friars, Newgate Street. Her head was parboiled and later placed on London Bridge. Her companions suffered the usual penalty for treason: they were hanged, drawn and quartered. They were disembowelled while still alive and their penis and scrotum placed in their mouths as a form of gag. Their heads were placed on the gates of the City of London. Perhaps the best summation of the event can be found in a letter written by Lord Lisle: "This Day the Nun of Kent with two Friars Observant, two monks and a secular priest, were drawn from the Tower to Tyburn and there hanged and beheaded. God if it be his pleasure have mercy on their souls." Hugh Rich did not share their fate. It is presumed he died in prison. The hanging of a woman was most unusual, for their normal mode of execution was by being burned at the stake.

Inevitably, it has to be asked whether she was a martyr or a pawn. If the former she received no plaudits from the Church as did More and Fisher. If a pawn in a larger plot she wrought havoc and destruction on those who chose to direct her in their treason. She brought down with her a number of worthy but perhaps naïve clerics. Only Edward Bocking can really be thought to have been a source for her revelations. Her convent was closed in 1535, the prioress died with a pension some years later. Syon Abbey suffered the same fate in 1539 as part of the general closure. The Marquess of Exeter and Lord Montague were beheaded in 1538, as was the Countess of Salisbury in 1541. Anne Boleyn, who could be seen as the cause of the whole gory business, was executed in 1536. The King was to have four more wives. The prophecy about sudden death did not occur.

It is perhaps sad that the one person about whom she prophesied, namely, the Princess Mary, did nothing to rehabilitate her considering that she had been so opposed to "the King's Great Matter" and had loyally championed Queen Catherine and herself. She had said of Mary, "That no man should fear but the Lady Mary should have succour and help enough, that no man should put her from her rights that she was born unto." Mary became Queen regnant in 1553, going down in English history by the name of "Bloody Mary".

Teresa Sanchez de Cepeda y Ahumada

In the early sixteenth century Spain had really only very recently become united. The year 1492 saw not only the discovery of America, but the end of the Moorish kingdom of Granada, making it part of the Spanish kingdoms of Aragon and Castile, completing the *reconquista*. At the same time Jews were required to become Christians or leave the country, and in 1502 Muslims had to make the same choice. The wealth of the Indies had yet to affect the country at all.

Teresa Sanchez de Cepeda y Ahumada, to become known to posterity as St Teresa of Avila, mystic and reformer, was born on 28 March 1515. Her father, Don Alonso, was of mixed ancestry – his family were *conversos* – that is persons of Jewish origin who had accepted Christianity. The fact that they were *conversos* was conveniently hidden, and might in part account for their removal from Toledo to Avila where the dubious family background could be conveniently and discreetly forgotten.

Teresa was the only daughter of her father's second marriage. By his first wife he had one daughter and two sons; by his second he had thirteen other children, twelve of them boys. As a small child she was much pampered, but early showed a strong sense of religiosity. At the age of seven she and her brother Rodrigo ran away from home determined to become Christian martyrs. They were to be frustrated in this project when they were apprehended by an uncle and returned to their parents. This adventure was commemorated in a poem by the seventeenth-century poet Richard Crashaw entitled, "A Hymn to the name and honour of the admirable saint Teresa".

When she was fourteen years of age her mother died. Her elder half-sister was already married, and, therefore, Teresa assumed responsibility for the domestic life of the large family. While outwardly she was untroubled, in fact she was lonely and isolated, despite the affection felt for her by her brothers. Her father, obviously a perceptive individual, recognised that she needed the support and guidance he could not give. To provide her with feminine society he decided that she should become a resident with the Augustinian sisters.

Teresa's initial reaction to her new life was not a particularly enthusiastic one. She found she missed the hustle and bustle of the family household, and the clamour of the brothers demanding her attention. However, she adjusted to conventual society and quickly became a favourite of the professed sisters. Gradually becoming less worldly in outlook, she began to wonder if she had a "vocation". Despite the affection she received from the nuns, she was not inclined – even if she did have a "vocation" – to join the Augustinian sisters.

In 1532 following a brief illness, her father sent her to reside with her half-sister and her husband. As she had few real responsibilities, she took to reading pious books the contents of which convinced her that the life of a nun was what she desired. Her father, on learning of her sentiments, disapproved strongly, declaring that he would only consent if she remained a layperson in his household until his demise. This seemingly arbitrary decision infuriated her and, refusing to be treated like a wayward child, she was determined to defy him. Accompanied by her brother, António, whom she had persuaded to assist her in her rebellion against parental authority, she left home and took up residence in the Carmelite convent in Avila. This independent act is perhaps an early indication that Teresa was perfectly capable of consulting her own wishes despite the reactions of others to the contrary. This act of flagrant disobedience soon began to weigh on her conscience and, as she was later to write, "I had no love of God to subdue my love for my father and kinsfolk." The former, of a loving and forgiving nature, accepted his daughter's decision, and in 1536 she was a fully professed nun.

Her life in the convent was agreeable. The sisters, some one hundred and eighty in number, really were residing in a sort of pension. They were allowed much personal freedom. There were, of course, the usual religious demands but they were not an undue burden. Teresa's father ensured his daughter was properly endowed with a sum, a sort of dowry, paid to the community. He undertook also to provide the necessary accoutrements for her own "cell" which included a guest room, a sleeping chamber, a kitchen and a small private oratory.

While more than adequately provided for in the creature comforts she was not overly satisfied with the spiritual life of the community. She attempted to resolve her personal questioning by fasting and spending hours in chapel. Becoming increasingly depressed, she was to have a breakdown. With the consent of her superiors she was permitted to leave the convent, and go to live with her sister as she had some years previously. After some months her general physical condition seemed to have improved, and she returned to the Carmelites.

Hardly had she rejoined the community than she had a relapse. She collapsed and went into a coma totally losing all consciousness. Her companions thought she was dead as she was without a sign of life. A grave was prepared; her father, however, would not let her be buried insisting that she still lived. His faith and his optimism were to be rewarded: after some four days, signs of consciousness were noted, and she emerged from the coma. She was to attribute her recovery to the intervention of St Joseph. Her general ill health continued, and for the next decade she was really a semi-invalid.

Her father's death in 1543 affected her deeply. She noted she felt "as if my very soul was being torn from me". Don Alonso's demise caused a family crisis. His children quarrelled over his estate. Teresa was called upon to mediate but without much success. The considerable wealth was dissipated in legal fees, and nobody profited except the lawyers. There was much bitterness, family regard vanished. Later four of Teresa's brothers were to die on the battlefield, generally unmourned by their siblings except for Teresa herself.

In her melancholy state she again sought consolation in prayer. She began to experience visions, which over the years were to become more frequent, and were to affect her life in a very direct fashion. For a short time, however, she was very uncertain about the visions. Were they merely imaginary, were they delusionary, were they consequences of her ill health? The other members of the community were equally uncertain about her soul. A priest to whom she turned for help was most unsympathetic, and declared that she was inspired by Satan. The upshot was that she in deep distress, wept copiously and became increasingly melancholy.

Rejected by her spiritual advisor she turned to the Jesuits. Earlier she had read Loyola's *Spiritual Exercises*. Her new confessor, Father Diego de Cetina, asserted that she was not in the hands of the devil after all. Restored by his counsel she gained a sense of equanimity and peace. She began to feel Christ was with her. The first of her so-called ecstasies occurred, which, like her visions earlier, were to be very significant. Her experiences were more and more frequent and more intense. Perhaps the most famous was "The Transverberation of Her Heart". This happened when she saw an angel of great beauty at her side. He carried a golden spear with a glowing tip. The spear penetrated her heart, and she felt much physical pain, but at the same time an intense love of God. Later St John of the Cross was to explain the event as "cauterising of the soul" and being not dissimilar to the stigmata as received by St Francis.

Generally speaking, the world at large regards conventual life as one of reasonable placidity, an ambiance of calm and repose. Such was not the situation in Avila. Teresa in ecstasy was not at all infrequent; in Chapel she was suddenly seen to be rigid, eyes closed and in a semi-unconscious state. Frequently she levitated, and the sisters had to grasp her firmly to prevent her rising to the ceiling. On at least one occasion she caused a crisis by going into rapture holding a frying pan. Her own comment on this was that "God walks among pots and pans!" She does not seem to have cared overly for the confusion her behaviour caused, for her God was merely manifesting Himself. Others may have had their doubts feeling that Teresa was indulging in extravagant and unseemly behaviour.

In the early autumn of 1560, she began to be increasingly critical of the existence enjoyed by the Carmelite sisters in Avila. She felt that a change was essential, that the easy life should be eschewed, and a more simple and puritanical conventual establishment should ensue. Her fellow sisters were irritated by her criticisms; they were inclined to feel that Teresa was setting herself above them, which in fact she was. Her independent and critical outlook was disturbing, and there were mutterings that she might properly be summoned by the Inquisition.

Undeterred by opposition, supported by a vision, and rescued by the rector of the Jesuit College with a house acquired by her family and with a benefactress from Toledo, a new foundation became a reality. It was not, however, until 1562 that with an apostolic rescript there was formal ecclesiastical approval. If the sisters of the Incarnation had been unsupportive, it was nothing as compared to the open hostility of the local citizens. They were vehemently opposed to a new charitable institution in the town. A lawsuit ensued. Teresa was not finally a full member of the new community for over a year, and it was only in March 1563 that she could join her "dear nuns". She formally took the name of Teresa of Jesus. Her activities in the reform were crowned with yet another vision when she was given a special indication of divine approbation by the Virgin. As was to be the case in almost all of her activities, Teresa could claim that God was showing his favour in those activities which she wanted to occur.

The reformed sisterhood were unlike those in the Incarnation. They had no real creature comforts, poor and inadequate food, rough habits, straw pallets and they were veiled at all times. Even when mass was said, the priest could not see their faces. Despite the austerity, there was no lack of potential postulants. Teresa decided that the community would be thirteen in number, to emulate Christ and the apostles. The sisters insisted that Teresa assume the office of prioress. Outwardly she was reluctant to do so, but probably felt that in accepting she was fulfilling the divine admonition that had given its support in the first instance. It is interesting to note that a divine vision was at hand on every occasion when she wanted to embark on a new and independent course of activity.

To regularise the reformed order Teresa wrote "The Constitution", outlining the rules of the community. This statement of how the sisters should live was to be extended in *The Way of Perfection*. This not only reiterated what had been already stated in The Constitution, but also dealt with prayer and contemplation in a religious life. Teresa had a nice sense of expressing herself. She concludes with the remark, "Well sisters our Lord seems not to want me to write any more, for although I had intended to go on, I can think of nothing to say."

From 1563 to 1567 her life was relatively peaceful. She seems to have resolved her conflict with her former convent, St Joseph's was firmly established and the local population had come to accept her reformed Carmelites. The ecclesiastical authorities gave outward indications that they approved of her efforts. Teresa was now aged fifty, and probably assumed that her adventures and her difficulties were at an end. Presumably, she would live at peace with God and her colleagues in her haven of St Joseph's.

However, this placid existence was to be rudely shortened by a new vision. As she was to say in 1566, "My Lord appeared to me in His casual way and said to me very lovingly as if He wished to bring me comfort, 'Wait a little daughter and thou shalt see great things!'" She was totally mystified by what she had been told. Hitherto, and probably quite conveniently, she had experienced visions which indicated divine approbation of some personal crusade of her own. She was thus fortified in knowing that her desire to bring a rigour to the religious life of the sisters at Avila, the intention to found a reformed convent and the rejection of unwelcome advice from clerics were all part of God's will. Did this recent admonition imply that she was to be called to convert the benighted heathen in the New World whose sad state of ignorance she had just been told? Alternatively was it a possible warning that she was about to experience a new conflict with authority? Such was not to be the case: the general of the Carmelite order approved of St Joseph's. Upon meeting him she noted, "I told him my story quite truthfully and simply for whatever the consequences. I am always inclined to do that way with prelates." What was to be required of her was an activity much to her liking, namely, to establish a new house in Medina del Campo. Despite initial local opposition as before, the new convent was supported by rich and influential patrons, including King Philip. With such support success was ensured.

Teresa was to become the symbol of a reformed spirit of Catholicism. She moved from place to place with a few female companions and a friar, Father Juan de Avila. Travel was difficult, for they, while peripatetic, attempted to live according to the rule. The nuns were veiled at all times, never speaking to their masculine companions. Only Teresa had contact with such persons. It was now that what might be defined as a masculine spirit fired her sense of action. It took control, stimulating her in a fashion that life, even a deep spiritual existence, could never do. Despite her frequent protestations to the contrary that she only desired the quiet life, this was only marginally true at best. She loved to direct, to be the centre of the action.

Her meeting with John of the Cross was most fortuitous. He had been ordained a priest in 1567. Teresa saw her mission to found a monastery based on the reformed Carmelites. John of the Cross, the new acolyte, was anxious to be directly involved with this project. In the winter of 1568 the two were to see a monastic community of great austerity as a result of their planning. A second establishment was formed soon after. One of the monks, Juan de la Miseria, an artist, painted the foundress's portrait. The subject of the painting was far from enthusiastic, noting to the artist, "God forgive you. You have made me ugly and bleary-eyed." Teresa and John of the Cross continued their peripatetic life. It must be noted that Teresa's existence was a very real contrast to what she ordained for her reformed Carmelites.

Not everyone bowed before her indomitable will and personality. The Princess of Eboli, the wife of a favourite of King Philip, invited Teresa to come to stay. The latter was disinclined to accept but another vision proposed the contrary. The princess wished to be the patroness of a new convent, whose sisters followed Teresa's rule. This plan might just have been possible, but the princess was exceedingly capricious, demanding that every detail, no matter how trivial, be determined by herself. The community was finally established, but was not a happy place. After the Prince of Eboli's death, his widow decided she would take up residence, and, when ensconced, demanded special privileges. A row ensued, she appealed to the king who ordered her back to her own palace. Frustrated she tried to have Teresa brought before the Inquisition but without success. She then actively persecuted the few nuns who remained in the convent until they finally fled leaving the place and all of the contents behind.

Teresa had really been a bystander because she had resisted all efforts of the Princess of Eboli to remain as her companion. Even so, the whole matter was not to her credit. She really did little to defend the poor sisters from the princess's unwanted attentions. Teresa retired to Toledo where she lived for a year and busied herself with a new opus, *Exclamation of the Soul to God*. She soon became bored with general inactivity; sedentary life, even when it involved literary endeavour, was not challenging. She started on her travels anew.

These journeyings stimulated her, but to the casual observer she and her entourage must have appeared most curious. She was generally accompanied by two or three friars, several devoted laymen and some pious young women who were destined to be denizens of her latest foundation. She was exceedingly well organised, and might well be deemed a highly effective if somewhat original tour director. So professional did she become that one observer noted that she seemed to have been going about on mules all of her life. These junketings had, of course, their own purposes. Firstly, they were chosen to visit places where she intended to found new convents and, secondly, to allow her to make visitations to previously established communities to ensure they were keeping the rule according to her specific directions. Even she, despite her not inconsiderable energy – she was now in her middle fifties – began to question her activities noting, "Again and again I have thought how much better I should be if I could stay safely at home." These self-doubts were quickly put aside for she was really totally disinclined to give up her peripatetic life.

This preferred existence came to a sudden end in 1571. The Convent of the Incarnation in Avila, her original community, had fallen into decline and, as critics would have it, real spiritual desuetude. There was a general laxity throughout the place – rather more so than when Teresa had joined the community. The regular observances of conventual life were performed in the most casual fashion, and the sisters, while neither depraved nor sexually promiscuous, were self-indulgent. The Carmelite Provincial decided a dose of discipline was in order and appointed Teresa as prioress. There was another vision, this time not necessarily in accord with her personal wishes, insisting that she obey her superior and the divine command sent her to Avila. The reaction of the sisters was one of real dismay, the prospect of a stern disciplinarian was most disagreeable but their protests were in vain. On 6 October 1571 Teresa assumed office amidst considerable pandemonium in the chapel.

A form of peace in due course ensued. Much of the laxity was halted, special privileges accorded to some of the sisters curtailed, and a degree of order in performing religious obligations demanded. Teresa was efficient enough, but she lacked the ability to delegate authority largely because she loved power and consequently was frequently rigid, inflexible and tactless in her dealings with the community. She was perceptive enough to know, however, that she had to be less abrasive in dealing with persons in authority.

Her sojourn at Avila was not entirely concerned with administration. She continued to have visions, go into ecstasy and raptures while having also personal conversations with God. These activities did not necessarily endear her to her fellow nuns who were often left with the feeling that Teresa alone was unduly privileged and not always generous in sharing her special position with the deity. On 18 November 1572 she received what to her was the ultimate sign of divine approbation. She was told she was truly the Bride of Christ. The sentiments of the other sisters in Avila were cordial enough but not necessarily much more than modified rapture.

In the autumn of 1574 she was able to give up office. Life in the Convent of the Incarnation was more orderly if less comfortable. Not everyone mourned her departure, perhaps most were glad to see her leave, but outwardly she had fulfilled the commands of her superiors. She betook herself off to her beloved St Joseph's where she was given a wonderful welcome, the shepherd reunited with the sheep.

Hardly had she settled that she was asked to form a new convent in Beas. She never seems to have been able to resist such requests, always feeling she was doing God's will, but her critics – and they were considerable in number – were of the opinion that she was totally unable to live the cloistered contemplative life that she assiduously demanded from others. Her critics also thought that with each new foundation her sense of self-importance was enhanced and that she became an increasingly powerful personage. Even her most enthusiastic advocates were forced to recognise that she was not averse to public acclaim under the right circumstances.

A new acolyte, Jeronian Gracian, entered her life. He became her personal confessor and the recipient of a considerable correspondence. Gracian had a very special place in that in one of her visions she and he had been united in a spiritual fashion. As she was to observe, "Blessed be He who has raised up someone to satisfy my needs and give me strength. . . ." In a sense Gracian, John of the Cross and Juan d'Avila were lovers, not in a physical sense, but they gave her the affection from the masculine sex that her dear nuns could not convey. These three men sustained her in such a way that she believed that against all odds she could accomplish anything. In these relationships she was really human; she was not just the Bride of Christ, the reformer of the Carmelites.

Free from administrative duties, the convent at Beas established, she resumed her travels. As Juan d'Avila complained bitterly as he was dragged along in her entourage: "The older she gets the more she travels!" At the same time she managed to write *The Interior Castle*, a summation of her mystical thoughts.

Thus far she had managed to survive all of the criticism upon herself both personally and the results of what she saw as her mission. However, at this juncture good fortune vanished: the Calced or Unreformed Carmelites went on the attack. Teresa was to be astonished at the ferocity of their efforts. She cried out, "The Calced go too far, they are blinded with rage . . . if only they stopped to think. . . ." Rational thought, as Teresa would have it, was far from their plans; they only wanted revenge for her disruptions of their peaceful life. She, herself, was placed under a form of house arrest. The provincial chapter of the Carmelites decided to reunite the two traditions with the Calced in control. Even Rome rejected her and the papal nuncio was particularly hostile.

One victim of this feud was poor John of the Cross. He was kidnapped by some Calced in December 1577 and held in a particularly disagreeable prison under very harsh conditions. He was singled out as being one of Teresa's closest friends and adherents. He refused to repudiate his patroness and luckily he managed to escape in the summer of 1578 to a Discalced community in southern Spain.

Although she had run afoul of the traditional members of her order, she was not entirely friendless. In due course the two branches of the Carmelites were ordered by royal decree to be separated. After four years of more or less house arrest, she was permitted to visit her various convents. Her good friend, Gracian, was elected provincial of the Discalced which ensured her reasonable protection in the future. She was not so unworldly as not to recognise that she personally had been a major cause of the crisis. Even so, essentially, she felt that mere mortal men were of no significance if they challenged and obstructed her work. She rejected the idea that any opinion contrary to her own had a real validity.

At the time of her release from confinement she was over sixty years of age, her close associates and friends were increasingly infirm or dead. She resumed residence in her beloved St Joseph's, but it was not a happy community. She assumed the office of prioress in an attempt to improve the situation, and nevertheless, despite some episcopal opposition, she continued to oversee the establishment of new foundations. At the time of her death she was directly responsible for seventeen new convents.

Although her health was not good, she insisted on continuing her journeying. Sedentary life and administrative obligations, despite her affection for St Joseph's, were not stimulating. When she reached Alba in the autumn of 1582 it was evident even to her that further travels were not to be. She herself noted, "My Lord, it is time to set out, may the journey be a propitious one and may Thy will be done." She further observed, "I do not know how we can grieve for those who go to a land of safety." From this expedition there would be no return. A final admonition, "I pray you [the Discalced sisters] for the love of God . . . to observe them [the Rule and the Constitutions] with the greatest possible perfection and to obey the superiors." She was determined her work should continue unaltered and in a sense rule from the grave. It is perhaps ironical that she insisted on obedience to authority when she herself had been quite willing to act according to her own personal inclination. She saw herself as the direct agent of divine command, and any objections to the contrary were expressions of the unenlightened and the ignorant. She died at Alba in 1582. She was sixty-seven years old.

Three days after her death she was buried but not embalmed. There was an immediate concern that St Joseph's would reclaim the body, which the sisters in Alba were determined to prevent. An armed guard was placed at the graveside which was also covered with a pile of rubble to make illegal excavation difficult.

However, despite these precautions her corpse was not allowed to rest in peace. Some nine months after her death, Gracian, her special friend and colleague in her mission, had the coffin disinterred. The remains were seen to be uncorrupted, and as a result the body was removed from the coffin, bathed and redressed. However, the corpse suffered from the first of a series of mutilations. Gracian had a hand cut off which was to be despatched to Avila. He himself retained one finger which was placed in a reliquary which thereafter he wore around his neck. (The finger was to have its own history. It was later in the possession of the Barbary pirates and had to be ransomed to ensure its return.) Three years later the coffin was again disinterred, further mutilations of the corpse followed. An arm was cut off and the body itself packed off to Avila. It did not rest there because in 1587, following a papal rescript, it was returned to Alba once again. The sadly mutilated body suffered further indignities. The "transverberated" heart, a right arm, a right foot and part of the lower jaw found their way to Rome. The left hand was sent to Lisbon.

Fingers are now to be found in Paris, Brussels and in the New World. The left hand, in a special reliquary, was to be stolen, but later was rescued and given to General Franco. He kept it by his bedside for forty years. Following his death, it was returned to the Carmelites. Teresa's portrait, painted in 1576, is to be found in a convent in Valladolid. The great statue by Bernini showing Teresa in ecstasy was carved in 1645 and is in Rome.

Despite all of her controversies with authority, both lay and ecclesiastical, all were to agree in due course that she was a truly major figure in western history. She was to become the patron saint of Spain and to join Catherine of Siena as a Doctor of the Church.

Teresa of Avila was a most complicated individual. Her voices and visions directed her life but undoubtedly allowed her to follow her own inclinations and to encourage her to act as she wished. She was not much concerned with public reaction, and was inclined to reject any idea contrary to her own. Opposition from others, be they persons in authority or not, she felt arose from either ignorance or stupidity. The ignorant she could inform, the stupid she would educate.

Inevitably, some questions arise. Did she challenge masculine authority being acutely aware that men do not understand women? This arose from personal experience as virtually the only female in a strictly masculine household as a child. She was not a social or political revolutionary, nor can she be considered a great theologian, she was rather a "deviating voice" who saw her mission quite clearly and was quite willing to risk displeasure from the church and society if she felt they were obstructive. She was always to be somewhat ambivalent about "the spirituals" and "the theologians" especially when they believed they had a "monopoly on truth and virtue" and attempted to impose their beliefs and ideas in a dictatorial manner. In truth she was both a free spirit and something of a feminist. She never presumed to assume a masculine role, but at the same time it must be recognised that she was not a particularly feminine person. Men like Gracian, Juan d'Avila and John of the Cross were colleagues and facilitators wooed through reason and not love. If she had doubts they were rarely expressed and throughout her active life she seemed to be governed by the adage, "I may not always be right, but I am never wrong!"

Jeanne Marie Guyon

If, as Père d'Avrigny observed, "les hommes font les hérésies, les femmes leur donnent cours et les rendent immortelles", then Jeanne Marie Bouvières de la Mothe – later Guyon – was an excellent embodiment of the aphorism. She was born in 1648, the daughter of Claude Bouvières de la Mothe. The de la Mothe family was large and scattered throughout France. For example, François de Salignac de La Mothe-Fénelon, the Archbishop of Cambrai who was to be one of Jeanne Marie's greatest intellectual supporters, and Antoine Arnauld, the ardent Jansenist who was to be one of her harshest critics, were her distant cousins.

Jeanne Marie was a frail child, and her mother, who seems to have been a rather self-indulgent person and unwilling to burden herself with a sickly little girl, packed her off at the age of two to be cared for by some Ursuline nuns. She remained with them for several months, and then, for reasons that are unexplained, she returned to her parental home. Her mother had not assumed any sudden maternal feelings, indeed quite the contrary, showing excessive affection for her son. The latter appears equally to have cared little for his sister, and it is said that on at least one occasion attempted to kill her. From this unhappy domestic situation – her father's sentiments regarding her are not known – she was rescued by the Duchesse de Montaubon who advised that the child be sent to a different convent; this time to a Benedictine establishment. She was now aged five, and seems to have been imbued with infant piety, revelling in the religious services, dressing up in nun's garb and being too obviously sanctimonious. Consequently, her contemporaries, like herself resident in the convent, found her tiresome and, when on one occasion she had expressed a desire to die a Christian martyr, they were only too ready to assist her to do so. Apparently she only just escaped by saying that she could not allow them to accomplish their desire until she had her father's permission to achieve such a holy death. She lived with the Benedictine nuns for a couple of years, and then quite suddenly, as before, her parents decided she should return home.

She had two older half-sisters, both of whom were Ursuline nuns, and almost as her previous removal from the Benedictines had been capricious, so was the decision that she would join her half-sisters. In this new convent once more she became assiduous in her chapel duties. So pious was she that she greatly impressed the widow of King Charles I of England, when his wife Henrietta Maria made a visit in 1656. When Jeanne Marie was ten the family removed her from the Ursulines, and once more she lived at home. This state of affairs continued only for a very short time, and she was then sent to reside in a Dominican convent. There does not appear to be any rational explanation for her parents' behaviour in constantly changing the religious orders chosen to be responsible for her upbringing.

It would seem that not only was Jeanne Marie a victim of family emotional abuse and parental rejection, but that she suffered from acute depressions and religious melancholia. Her unhappy mental state is hardly surprising for she does not seem to have felt at home or at ease anywhere. All of these sentiments she recounts in some detail in her autobiography. Despite her generally gloomy view of the world, she seems only to have been somewhat happy when present at mass. Evidently even at a young age she had considerable comprehension of the more abstruse aspects of theological abstractions.

When she was fifteen her life was radically altered. From a rural estate in Montargis she and her family moved to Paris. The city was deemed to be the centre of French life and King Louis XIV who still resided in the capital was the focal point of society. The Fronde was at an end, the age of absolute monarchy was in the making. The young daughter of Claude de la Mothe made an excellent impression on everyone who made her acquaintance. She was demure enough in manner, but at the same time she had intelligence and spirit. Moreover, she was thought to be handsome, not necessarily beautiful, but elegant in deportment and manner. In sum it could be said that the ugly duckling had become a swan.

She was now aged sixteen and her father, deciding that she should marry, selected for a son-in-law Jacques Guyon. The latter was some 22 years older than his prospective bride, but as he was wealthy the disparity in age was to Claude de la Mothe of little account. Socially perhaps the bride-elect was rather more aristocratic than her fiancé, and later she was to say that it was only on her parents' command that she consented to marry beneath her rank in society.

Jacques Guyon was essentially a very decent man, a good and faithful husband and of a thoughtful and generous nature. His assets were outweighed, however, by his unfortunate decision that he and his young wife should reside under the same roof as his mother. The elder Madame Guyon evidently had a rather despotic character, being also somewhat tactless and showing an unfeeling attitude towards her daughter-in-law whom she apparently regarded as an unwelcome interloper. She attempted to break the young woman's spirit, and treated her as a wilful child. In such a household there was no intellectual stimulation and little congenial society, all a very real contrast to the lively and engaging de la Mothe establishment.

In the second year of her marriage she gave birth to her elder son Armand Jacques Guyon. In due course she was to have two more children, a second son and a daughter. Having a family brought her little pleasure, and did not add much to her rather dreary existence. She began to suffer from deep depressions followed by a physical collapse, so serious was her general condition that she was thought to be near death. Gradually she recovered, and, turning to religion for a solace, she became very assiduous in her attendance at church hearing mass almost daily. She abandoned what little social intercourse she had in general, and occupied her time reading pious books. In the summer of 1668 she experienced what she would ultimately define as an inner life. However, her excessive piety bored and irritated her husband.

In an attempt to improve his domestic situation Jacques Guyon decided to house his wife and children in an establishment separate from his mother's residence. The new arrangement was generally a happier situation, and his wife, in particular, appears to have gained a more balanced perspective about herself.

In an age which often appears to have been very rational in thought, mysticism was not unfashionable. Jeanne Marie Guyon began to express these mystical feelings in poetry. Already she had heard a special "voice", which she deemed to be from God offering guidance in her personal life. For example, after having been afflicted with smallpox and having lost her good looks, the "voice" apparently said to her, "If I [in this instance God] would have thee fair I would have left thee as thou wert."

At this time she became acquainted with Father François La Combe with whom she began an extensive correspondence. She said of his friendship that it brought her "the peace of God". Her happier mental and emotional situation resulted in a rather more congenial domestic existence. At the same time a third son was born, replacing the one who had recently died, and this child was to become the favourite.

The elder son was much influenced by his grandmother, and, in his mother's opinion, was never a truly sympathetic individual. Increasingly Jeanne Marie Guyon felt that she was a bride of Christ, she had come to believe that inner prayer alone had value and with it sanctification by faith. She began to think that God had selected her for his own special purposes. In 1676 her husband died; his estate was bequeathed to the children but with a generous financial provision for his widow.

Because of her obligations to her two sons and a daughter, she could not act as she wished, namely, to retire to a convent. Her spiritual life as a lay person continued to be directed by La Combe and their correspondence became more frequent. Another priest, Claude Martin, also became a guiding figure. His mother, Sister Marie de l'Incarnation, had entered a convent and had later become a missionary in Canada.

Martin proposed that in spite of her domestic obligations she should change her way of life totally. He suggested that she should retire to Savoy, that part of France bordering on Switzerland, and assist in the mission dealing with the *Nouveaux Convertis*, that is the Huguenots who had been reconciled to Catholicism. Accepting his idea she more or less abandoned her sons – they were left in the hands of tutors and servants – and, accompanied by her daughter and three female companions, she left Paris in the summer of 1681. She took up residence in Gex living in a convent with La Combe to act as her spiritual director. It was at this time that she really began what was to be her role in life, namely, that of an evangelist of sorts. Her message was simple, it was the spirituality of Quietism. La Combe had already apparently adopted a similar theological stance. She and he were to be closely involved for the next five years.

Her activities did not please the local bishop who recognised that she was well enough intentioned but essentially dangerous, preaching questionable doctrine. He tried various ways to silence her but without success initially. Moreover, La Combe encouraged her to continue her evangelistic activities. His support of her gave rise to gossip, and there were those who believed they were lovers. However, there is no real evidence to support such a calumny.

When not preaching or holding prayer meetings, she busied herself with her writings, in particular *Moyen Court*. She was trying to define her own position within the church, she was, she believed, to be *in* the church but not *with* it, accepting its form but not its spirit. Increasingly ill regarded by the local authorities, she and La Combe were expelled by the bishop from his diocese. The couple moved to

Italy accompanied by her daughter and some domestics. It was probably at this time that she became acquainted with the writings of Miguel de Molinos.

In his book, *A Spiritual Guide*, he rejected the formal ceremonies of the mass preferring rather to rely on faith alone, maintaining the doctrine of present and effective sanctification. His teachings were adjudged to be heretical, and he was silenced in 1685 by imprisonment. Jeanne Marie Guyon's writings expressed similar ideas, but for the moment she was not prohibited from expounding them. After a relatively brief sojourn in Italy, she returned to France, and once again she counselled the penitent, comforted the sinners and preached at what she called her conferences. As previously, she encountered opposition for her activities which it appears was partly inspired by the fact that she was a woman. She observed somewhat wryly that "they [her opponents] were grievously chagrined that a *woman* should be so flocked to and sought after."

On the advice of La Combe she began to write her *Autobiography*. In this curious book she gives the impression that she is some sort of saint. She says she confronted Satan who shook her bed and rearranged her furniture. For penance she rolls in nettles, puts stones in her shoes, sucks on wormwood, and kneels on snakes to show no fear. She knows through her "voice" that she is assured of salvation without recourse to purgatory. Among her attributes she declares that she has the power to heal the sick and to cast out devils. She felt unappreciated, however, since she was not taken seriously enough in her claims. She certainly was paranoic and suffered from persecution mania. Her mysticism is overlaid with a lively imagination. She believed that she personally said nothing, that she had no personal ideas, everything was God: "I find no more *me*, there is no longer other *I* but God!" She is the star-crowned woman of the Apocalypse. She feels no need to pray to the saints because she has become one. This curious mélange of ideas found little support from the more orthodox in the community.

After returning to Paris she cultivated the society of *les bas bleus*. In their company she was well regarded not only for her obvious piety but also for her apparent intellectual attainments. While she was enjoying the applause and approbation of society, her friend La Combe was not so fortunate. He was to be arrested for advocating the heresies of Molinos and imprisoned in Lourdes Castle. He went insane and died in gaol some 27 years later. His protégé Jeanne Marie Guyon, despite his pleas, categorically refused to visit him. It has been suggested that she was scandalised by La Combe's confessions about sexual peccadilloes possibly implicating herself.

Her half-brother, the Abbé de la Mothe, wishing to extricate her from the heretical circles embodied by La Combe, proposed to assume the role of her spiritual director. She rejected the plan; to silence her he, therefore, had her placed under arrest. Her stay with the Sisters of the Visitation was somewhat dreary and generally uncomfortable. Through the influence of friends at court, and despite the personal reservations of King Louis XIV regarding her views, she was released after eight months incarceration. Once free she moved again in cultivated society and the intellectual world where she became friendly with Madame de Maintenon, the King's mistress, and enjoyed the patronage of several prominent ladies of the court. As a protégé of Madame de Maintenon, she became an habitué of St Cyr, the academy for the instruction of young ladies, and she became a frequent visitor and a popular guest. Madame de Maintenon, who had converted to Roman Catholicism from a Calvinistic Protestant family, found her new friend's views sympathetic. Unfortunately Jeanne Marie Guyon used the opportunity of such a patroness's approbation to indoctrinate the young women in her special views of prayer. Such ideas were unorthodox and her activities were bound to have unhappy consequences.

At this juncture her kinsman, François Fénelon, entered her life. His career and her own were to be intertwined in an intimate fashion to the disadvantage of both. Fénelon was a most gracious and charming individual, thoughtful, intelligent and generous spirited. He held the post of the principal instructor to the young Duc de Bourgogne, the grandson of King Louis XIV. Fénelon seems to have been much impressed by Madame Guyon and, although he did not accept her ideas completely, he was convinced of her sincerity, and that she spoke the language of the mystics.

Just what were her ideas? Firstly, perfection consists in a continual act of contemplation. Secondly, a soul that has reached perfection is no longer obliged to specific acts and everything resulting from personal industry is contrary to perfect repose in God. Thirdly, such a soul is indifferent to everything relating to the body and soul and to all physical things. Finally, in a situation of perfect contemplation the soul must repel all distinct ideas, even the attributes and mysteries of Christ. The final analysis of such views were that *pur amour* led inevitably to the surrender of any ideas of salvation. Orthodoxy being concerned for hope rejected this interpretation as being contrary to

God's will.

It has been said that Madam de Maintenon, for reasons of her own and disliking the friendship of Fénelon and Jeanne Marie Guyon, requested the great preacher, Bishop Jacques-Bénigne Bossuet, to intervene. Unlike Fénelon, he read everything that she had written; he was scandalised by the heterodoxy expressed in her writings. Moreover, hearing reports of her conversations at St Cyr he decided that she was a dangerous individual. Louis XIV now intervened, and appointed a commission of three, namely, Bossuet, de Noailles, then bishop of Chalons, but later to become Archbishop of Paris, and Tronson, the superior of St Sulpice, to determine whether or not she was a heretic. Her *Autobiography* and her *Moyen Court* were closely studied. While a decision was in the process of being made, she and Fénelon seem to have signed a document that generally repudiated Quietism. Evidently Bossuet had his doubts about her apparent retractions but did not regard her as dangerous.

By now she was totally ill-regarded by Madame de Maintenon and the King was thoroughly alarmed by what he had been told. Friends seem to have warned her of her position, and she went into hiding in Paris, but late in December 1697 she was found by the police and arrested. Noailles, who earlier had been on the commission to read her writings, now wrote to Madame de Maintenon, "What do you think we should do with this woman and her friends and writings?" A decision was not long in the making. King Louis XIV ordered that she be confined to the fortress of the Château de Vincennes. Her imprisonment was much more restrictive than had been her stay in the convents early in 1695. She could no longer receive guests nor communicate with the world. The heretic was silenced. Her only company was her maid.

Her associate Fénelon also fell under royal displeasure. He lost his position in the household of the Duc de Bourgogne and was exiled to Cambrai. He was really only a crypto-Quietist, but he probably did believe that Jeanne Marie Guyon's method of prayer was well suited to bring an individual near to God. His writings were scrutinised by the Church; he was to be criticised in part for what he had said but not over harshly. Nevertheless his public career was at an end and he remained exiled from Paris and royal circles.

After some six months in Vincennes, she was moved to Vaugiraud and then transferred to the Bastille. She does not appear to have repented or recanted. The misfortunes of Fénelon and the young ladies of St Cyr apparently left her unconcerned. Even her son experienced the royal wrath by being dismissed from the army. Poor mad La Combe was brought into service by the authorities. He sent a letter – probably forged – demanding that she recognise her sinful and disobedient state. Bossuet continued his hostility, feeling that she had acted dishonestly when she had signed a statement that she repudiated her views a few years earlier. He said of her that she was *une femme dont les lumières et aient courtes, le mérite si léger, les illusions si palpables*.

She remained in the Bastille until 1702, and upon her release she was banished to Blois. She was under a sort of house arrest in the custody of her son. She lived until 1717 in declining health but continuing to see disciples and writing letters.

She has been called half a saint and half a lunatic. She was unwise in her behaviour, and had little real humility. She was somewhat intellectually dishonest. She had no doubts about herself, and always thought she was absolutely right in all that she did and believed. She pretended to be able to do nothing herself; only God acted through her. She was complacent and immoderately self-centred. Her autobiography is an eccentric work and full of falsehoods. She believed that she was sanctified not by her virtues like the saints but rather by God Himself.

Apart from her considerable correspondence with men like La Combe and Fénelon, her principal writings were her *Autobiography*, the *Explanation of the Canticle of Canticles* and the *Moyen Court*. Her *Spiritual Torrents* was never published in her life time. She found readers in countries other than France, and Protestants were often inclined to view her as the victim of the bigotry of Louis XIV and the Roman Catholic Church. The condemnation of the Quietest movement had a deleterious effect for many years on the development of mystical spirituality in the Catholic world.

Selina, Countess of Huntingdon

In the eighteenth century aristocratic families were not generally known for their piety. Indeed, while quite prepared to attend services in the local parish church, they did not favour what they were to call "enthusiasm". The Anglican Church was part of the accepted social order, the services were to be conducted according to the Book of Common Prayer and all was to be performed in a decorous fashion. To be sure some members of the "lower orders" did indulge themselves on occasion in a manner and a fashion which deviated from the approved code of behaviour. Therefore, when an aristocrat acted in a fashion to challenge the accepted and traditional role there was considerable surprise and in some instances consternation and even real hostility. Lady Selina Shirley, later Countess of Huntingdon, was one such individual.

Lady Selina Shirley was born in 1707 on the thirteenth of August; later she was to celebrate her birthday on the twenty-fourth of the month following the adoption of the Gregorian calendar. She was the second daughter of Washington Shirley, Earl Ferrers. Two of her cousins were to gain some notoriety; the first was Laurence Shirley, the fourth Earl Ferrers, who murdered his steward and was hanged for the crime, being the last peer to suffer the death penalty. The second was Walter Shirley, a cleric in Ireland, who was a supporter of "methodism" much to the disapproval of the episcopate, and who gained some fame as a writer of evangelical hymns that were on occasion used in the chapels organised by his cousin; one such hymn was composed on the occasion of the departure of some missionaries bound for America with the opening line, "Go destined vessel, heavenly freighted go!"

The Shirley family were known for their litigious and umbrageous behaviour. Fathers disinherited sons; the latter quarrelled with their mothers, and were rude and disagreeable to their siblings. Dowries and other forms of settlement were often unpaid for years because of lawsuits that were long outstanding. In some ways they embodied all of the more notorious characteristics of the Irish ascendancy as imagined in England.

Washington Shirley and his wife Anne, the daughter of John Elliott, had separate households. The two elder daughters, Elizabeth and Selina, lived with their father in Ireland while the youngest girl, Mary, resided with her mother in France. After the formal separation the older two had only the most casual of relations with the latter. Because of the complicated domestic arrangement Selina received a very rudimentary education. This was to be seen in the fact that she never seems to have learned how to spell or to understand the art of paragraphing or punctuation. Her orthography was also rather inadequate. But this lack of formal instruction does not appear to have restricted her intellectual interests or the ability in later life to manage the family estates and the chapels with considerable success.

When she was aged twenty-one she married Theophilius Hastings, the ninth Earl of Huntingdon. It is unclear whether it was an arranged marriage or a real love match. Indeed, whatever the origin, they were to be a most happy couple. Everyone on both sides of the family was, for once, united in giving their general approbation. The groom's family, incidentally, were as fond of going to law as was the bride's. Indeed, at the very moment of the nuptials the two families were involved in a suit against each other.

The Huntingdons were to have seven children, four sons and three daughters; two of the boys and two of the girls were to die young. The eldest son, Francis, was ultimately to succeed to his father's title but both he and his youngest brother predeceased their mother, only Elizabeth, her daughter, managed to outlive her. The family resided in London in a house belonging to William Kent, the architect; they also had a sort of pied-à-terre in the environs called Enfield Chase and a "place" in the country called Donnington Park in Leicestershire.

Although Selina Huntingdon's education had been inadequate, she insisted that such should not be the case with her own children. All of the boys were sent to Westminster while the girls had governesses and tutors of the highest calibre. Indeed, her daughters were to learn Latin, Greek and even Hebrew as well as the usual subjects of instruction. All of the children were required to read the Bible regularly, to attend church services, and to give the parents an analysis of the sermon.

Her interests in the world of the Church were very evident even in her early married life. She quickly gained a reputation as a lady bountiful providing aid to those she deemed to be "the deserving poor". She was an enthusiastic supporter of the Society for the Promotion of Christian Knowledge, bought bibles and prayer books to give to "the lower orders". Her interest in "Methodism" arose through the influence of her husband's favourite half-sister, Lady Betty, who was very friendly with the two Wesleys and George Whitfield. She was also quite intimate with members of the Moravian Church, and their tracts were read with enthusiasm by Selina Huntingdon, whose new-found "enthusiasm" dismayed and disturbed her family and some of her friends. They tried to persuade her husband to curtail her somewhat excessive zeal but in vain. He was himself not immune to the "enthusiasm" and when a protégé of Lady Betty made the couple's acquaintance, he found it easy to persuade them to "betake [themselves] to the Life of Religion". Their new friends, the Moravians and the Methodists, became very much part of their lives, and they were to be very supportive following the demise of two of their sons and Lady Betty.

Donnington Park was the setting for visits by the pious and virtuous. Many clerics enjoyed the Huntingdon's hospitality and, in return, conducted church services preaching learned sermons for their host and hostess. Among those who were visitors were John Wesley and George Whitfield, two men who were to be very influential in the life of Selina Huntingdon.

The Huntingdons became more closely associated with the Methodists following the marriage of Lady Margaret Hastings to Benjamin Ingham. The later, an Oxonian, was an early adherent of John Wesley whom he had known at Oxford. Ingham's life was largely that of an evangelical – incidentally he was also a protégé of Lady Betty – and by virtue of his piety became a very real and directly influence on the Huntingdons. The consequence was that Ingham used his relationship to have his friends assist youthful clerics who were Methodists – still officially Anglican – to be permitted to preach in neighbouring parish churches.

At this juncture it was not the intentions of John Wesley and his like-minded friends to break with the Established Church. Rather they wanted to re-animate the dormant and somewhat torpid spirit of the Church of England. They were to emphasise the Protestant character of the Church and to utilise "exhorters", as their preachers were called, to bring "the good news" to the world at large, very much in the tradition of the dissenting sects. However, unlike these bodies, the tenor of the preachings was not Calvinistic in tone but rather Arminian. Predestination was rejected, and Wesley himself advocated "free will and universal and sufficient grace" rather than Calvin's limited "effective grace".

Initially, Selina Huntingdon appears to have accepted John Wesley's position. For a time she was a regular attendant at his chapel in London at Fetter Lane, and was a supporter when he chose to sever his relations with the Moravians. Ultimately, she was to reject his Arminianism and more or less sever all connections with him, however, this disruption does not seem to have altered her friendship with Charles Wesley whom she continued to regard favourably. Her chief spiritual advisor over the years was to be George Whitfield; he saw her not infrequently during his sojourns in London.

Her religiosity increased following the demise of her two sons in 1743, then with the death of a sister a year or so later and that of her husband in 1746. The last had been in ill health for some time, but nobody, least of all he, had considered his illness to be mortal. The estate was in considerable disarray; Selina Huntingdon had to go to law to get the legal authority to manage the money and property for her three remaining children. The deceased was buried at Ashby-de-la-Zouch, another family property. The memorial inscription was written by Lord Bolingbroke, a curious choice perhaps since he was a free thinker. However, it may well be, to paraphrase Doctor Johnson, that when one writes a lapidary inscription one is not on oath.

For the next decade her chief responsibility was in the management of the estate. Even after her son came of age, he allowed and encouraged his mother to continue in her position of authority. Finally, she was permitted to retire from these duties. She handed the management of Donnington Park to its owner, and she herself retired to a dower house where she resided with her younger son and surviving daughter. The household also consisted of several of her late husband's unmarried sisters. While she had been involved with the family property her enthusiasm for "the Methodists" continued unabated. She also maintained an active correspondence with various evangelicals, both Anglican and dissenting, and with pious people such as William Law. She attempted to convince members of her own social class of the virtues of Methodism. These attempts were often received coolly or outright rebuffed. Lady Buckingham's answer to one such appeal will serve as a good example.

> I thank your Ladyship for information concerning Methodist preaching; their doctrines are most repulsive and strongly tinctured with impertinence . . . as it is monstrous to be told that you have a heart as sinful as the common wretches that crawl on the earth. This is highly offensive and insulting – I cannot but wonder that your Ladyship should relish any

sentiments so much at variance with high rank and good breeding.

When George Whitfield had returned from the American colonies to England in 1748, she appointed him her chaplain. The rights to appoint chaplains were strictly laid down by the order of precedence, but being the widow of a peer she came to the curious conclusion that she had the right to appoint as many chaplains as she wished. Consequently, a number of youthful clerics, suspected of methodistical beliefs, were to find a refuge in her household. By 1750 or so she had committed herself totally to the Calvinism of Whitfield. In so doing she became an indirect part of the dissenting tradition, but nevertheless at the same time she continued to regard herself an Anglican.

Ever optimistic, she always hoped that she could reform society. Apparently she had some modest successes in that on one occasion she persuaded such free thinkers as Bolingbroke, Chesterfield and Hume to listen attentively, at least outwardly, to the sermons of Whitfield. She even imagined that Frederick, Prince of Wales, who died in 1757, was "on the road to Damascus" and conversion to a "better life". Whitfield is reported to have had similar delusions; he wrote to her, "As there seems to be a door opening for the nobility to hear the Gospel. . . . I will be at your Ladyship's and want to know your orders. . . . Oh that my God may be with me and make me humble." One of her protégés after praising her efforts noted, "I love to pray for your Ladyship, I feel a sweetness upon my soul whenever I do". She even almost convinced herself that the establishment might be enlightened enough to make George Whitfield a bishop. Perhaps this was not a complete impossibility, as her son was to hold various offices in the government in the Whig interest, and it might just happen that he could convince his colleagues to gratify his mother's dearest wish.

After her daughter's marriage to the Earl of Moira and the death of her younger son, she decided to move to Clifton near Bristol. By so doing she could renew a direct contact with Charles Wesley – she had been supplementing his salary for some years – whom she found personally very sympathetic. At this same time she became intimate with four women, Catherine Edwin, Ann Greenfield, Elizabeth Shrine and Anne Barlow, all of whom were to be intimately involved with the Methodist Movement and who were very assiduous in attending church services under its auspices. In addition she became acquainted with a Moravian group in Bristol, indeed, some of her friends were apprehensive that she might actually become a member of the community, but she did not do so, remaining an Anglican. She saw the Anglican Church as all-encompassing, and even tried to persuade her Moravian friends to abandon their independence.

Taking advantage of her social position and her obvious wealth, she went so far as to try a set up a council to reconcile the Arminians and the Calvinists, the Moravians and the Anglicans. While her efforts were doomed to failure, it was evident that she was a commanding figure in the city. She did manage at least to ensure that outward hostility among the various groups was less noticeable, and that at least in her company she would brook no public wrangling.

She evidently saw herself in a unique role. She was a distributor of largesse to a wide circle, she continued to her use influence wherever possible to promote the careers of young persons, persuading sympathetic bishops to ordain them as priests. She was not unaware, of course, that excessive enthusiasm was not always well regarded by the episcopate. The bishops generally wanted stable and traditional individuals that would not disturb the social order. She had a retinue of chaplains; at one time five at least were in her direct employ. Her personal chapel saw the communion service performed on a daily basis – highly unusual in the eighteenth century. However, these chaplains were not unlike upper servants to her mind, and were generally referred to only by their surnames. They gained no deference from her by being in holy orders, and indeed even Whitefield wrote of her in the most humble – indeed humiliating – terms.

In a real sense all of this was a prologue to the ultimate establishment of her so-called "connexion". It did not come about fully formed, it gradually evolved. Her first chapel, as a separate building from her house, was erected in Brighton in 1760. The proceeds necessary for its construction came from the sale of her jewellery. Other chapels were to be constructed over the next few years in towns frequented by the gentry and substantial middle class, and were to be found in Bath, Tonbridge and London. Officially the chapels were as adjuncts to the local parish churches. Their purpose was as a place for preaching and evangelising. Supposedly, they were to be self-supporting, but this was not always the case. They, or rather the "exhorter" who was in charge, were subsidised by their benefactress or by another sympathetic and wealthy individual. Actually by controlling the financial situation, Selina Huntingdon's wishes always prevailed.

The most famous chapel that she established was in Spa Fields in London. It was erected in 1779. A local clergyman opposed its erection. She, on the other hand, refused to desist in her plan, convinced of her right to have as many personal chapels as she had chaplains. A lawsuit ensued in a church court in London, and the decision went against her. Thereafter, the chapels existed under the Toleration Act and her chaplains took the necessary oaths as dissenting ministers.

The chapels had mixed receptions. In some instances they were welcomed, and the "exhorters" were praised and commended by the laity. In other cases – as at Spa Fields – the "exhorters" were the objects of much hostility and the local parish clergy saw them as dangerous rivals preaching radical ideas. One thing quickly became evident: that with the establishment of each new chapel there were an insufficient number of individuals to conduct the services. This lack of personnel led to her next major act, namely to establish her own training college. She vastly enjoyed being in control, her relationship with the chapels was most fulfilling in that she had an occupation. Managing the chapels replaced her activities on the estate at Donnington.

While many of the young men whom she supported were grateful to her for their stipends, at the same time some inevitably found her dictatorial manner not easy to accept. Moreover, the colleges at Oxford and Cambridge showed a certain reluctance to be a ready source of potential chaplains. St Edmund's Hall at Oxford was one of the very few such colleges which was openly supportive; others were at best neutral and on occasion openly hostile. The obvious solution was her own training college. While those persons who were to become the student body were not *per se* eligible for ordination in the Church of England, they could be trained to preach sermons that were acceptable to her particular requirements. A theological college of sorts was established at Trefuca Isaf in North Wales.

In 1767 Trefuca House was leased; certain alterations were needed and the place was essentially rebuilt according to Selina Huntingdon's own designs. The building was generally enlarged, rooms were added for the students, there was a chapel in mock gothic; some public reception rooms ornamented with scriptural passages and other edifying commentary. There was also a sort of suite for herself when she came to stay, which she did relatively frequently. Her prospective visits could inspire such remarks, "When will your Ladyship revive us with another visit? What blessings did the Lord shower on us the last time you were here." The entire domestic staff was appointed by the benefactress herself, another example of her sense of control. There was to be a housekeeper, a cook, a handy man and two women who acted either as cleaners or laundresses.

The actual instruction was to be done by two preceptors: William Fletcher was formally named as president and Joseph Benson as headmaster. Somewhat oddly the latter was appointed on the advice of John Wesley, with whom Lady Huntingdon was still not on the best of terms. This appointment was ultimately to be not very satisfactory because of the conflicts between her Calvinism and Benson's Arminianism. The college was formally opened on the occasion of the patroness's birthday, namely 28 August 1768. She and four female friends were in residence as was George Whitfield, who preached to the assembled company. Initially, there were seven students, who were enrolled for three years. After completing their studies they might apply for ordination in either the Church of England, assuming they could find a bishop who was prepared to perform the necessary rites, or become ministers in any dissenting denomination. Her particular intention was for the young men to serve in her chapels as much as possible.

In the first few years there were a number of visitations by clergy sympathetic to the general ethos of the college. Lady Huntingdon herself acted as a sort of hostess, and it was evident that her own role was of considerable importance. Naturally the whole place was evangelical in tone, simple and homely. The visitors generally were invited to give sermons or homilies for the edification of the staff, the students and various friends. Despite the somewhat formal relations between the Wesley brothers and Lady Huntingdon, they were received with cordiality initially when they came to visit.

This cordiality soon evaporated. John Wesley in particular found himself completely out of harmony with the place. He feared that the institution was almost heretical, with overtones of Quietism. He deplored the idea too that a sinner, and this was everyone, should await salvation without taking positive steps to seek it, in accord with his Arminian beliefs. He also though that Antinomianism was part of the foundress's ideas. He suspected too after conversing with some of the students that they were not Trinitarians but crypto-Unitarians, or that more heretically they believed in Universalism. An inevitable rupture ensued. Lady Huntingdon required the students to disavow John Wesley and his ideas. Failure to do so meant immediate expulsion from the college. Only her views were acceptable. Joseph Benson found this authoritarian attitude unacceptable and resigned his post. His departure was evidently not regretted by Lady Huntingdon. How the students really felt about her demands is not known.

The students were essentially totally beholden to her. Many came from quite impoverished backgrounds; she provided everything for them, gave them pocket money, paid all of the essential expenses of the establishment, and even bought the clothing for the young residents. She had a sort of maternal concern for them but like many matriarchs she expected total and absolute obedience, and was not inclined to tolerate any form of intellectual or social independence.

The curriculum consisted of the classical languages and theology. The course of studies was periodically interrupted at the whim of the foundress when she required their services to preach in her chapels. This capriciousness was far from being beneficial to the students. Moreover, the sermons these young men delivered were not infrequently paraphrased restatements of those preached by visiting clerics. It was all too obvious that the students were not prepared intellectually for what they were required to do, and the content of their preaching left a good deal to be desired. Zeal alone was really insufficient. The college was essentially an extension of the patroness's family. William Fletcher, the president, accepted the situation for six years and then he too resigned. He was replaced with a candidate more amenable in his attitude.

On his death in 1770 George Whitfield left his friend his American property. This consisted in the main of an orphanage at Bethesda near Savannah in Georgia. The buildings and some 500 acres became her personal possession. The whole place was in poor condition. It was badly administered, not so much as corrupt as incompetent. She took a firm hand, dismissed the staff and appointed individuals who were her protégés. She selected a few young men to go to America, certain in her own mind they would never challenge her authority. Several who were chosen did not wish to leave England, but she gave them no choice. They were evidently too timid or too cowed to decline. When they arrived in Bethesda they were acutely unhappy, but as in other situations under Lady Huntingdon's aegis her wishes were the only ones that mattered.

Shortly after her protégés arrived in Bethesda, the orphanage was destroyed by fire. Lady Huntingdon proceeded to send about £10,000 to rebuild it. The orphanage was always to be a financial drain and the whole establishment was generally unprofitable. What money was earned seems to have come from the slaves that were part of the inheritance from Whitfield. Lady Huntingdon's attitude towards slavery was unclear, but it may well be that she thought this was not significant. To her, life hereafter was more important than bondage here on earth. The outbreak of the American Revolution caused further problems. The property was not confiscated by the local authorities, and after the war she re-assumed control. It must be said that Whitfield did her no favour in bequeathing her his colonial lands. It should be noted that in 1809, a decade or so after her death, the place was abandoned. To be realistic all her efforts to administer and control the institution were in vain. She had one more American project. She wrote to George Washington, whom she always considered a kinsman, since her father had been named Washington, proposing the establishment of a community with selected emigrants, who were to be guided by her own precepts. Nothing came of the idea, and probably George Washington never considered it a serious proposition.

Although she had established a number of chapels, until the day she died she did not see herself as anything but an Anglican. The trustees of her college were all members of the Church of England and the services in the chapels were conducted according to the Book of Common Prayer. Only rarely did she permit a dissenting minister to preach in one of her chapels. After the building of the Spa Fields chapel she was forced to recognise that she had in actuality created an independent and separate church. What followed was to be designated as "The Countess of Huntingdon's Connexion".

As the years progressed the college and its students continued to command her principal attention. The student body, some ten or so per year, were to be guided and directed by her in all things, physical, moral and spiritual. She took a particular interest in their sermons. "The more scriptural and simple", she wrote, "to the heart the better applying the Facts and [staying] there" was what she required. Whenever she visited Trefuca she saw the students collectively and individually and determined which ones were to go on circuit. Those who attempted to evade her commands were sternly admonished, and they were queried as to their commitment to their calling. Excessive "enthusiasm" such as speaking in tongues or whirlings and dancing in an uncontrolled fashion were frowned upon. Possession by the Holy Spirit in such a way could only lead, if continued, to expulsion from the college.

The preceptors were required to give her regular reports on the students' academic progress. She did not hesitate to chide the young men if she thought they were being indolent in their studies. In addition to the accounting of student life, the farm was well managed and the domestics also were closely supervised. Until a year before she died she alone was firmly in control. Like Pitt the Elder, she could rightly say, "Being responsible, I will direct!" She liked power and as she became older she became even more authoritarian.

In 1790 she finally agreed to make some other arrangements for the college and the chapels. To ensure the survival of the college she created "The Apostolic Society", the membership of which was to be selected initially by herself. They and the students were to sign "The Fifteen Articles of the Connexion". The new leadership was to continue Lady Huntingdon's general practice of sending the students, now some twenty or so a year, to preach on a regular basis and all were to adhere to her Calvinistic convictions.

Following her death the college was reorganised and established at Cheshunt. The students now generally ceased to be Anglicans and were ordained in non-Conformist denominations. It later moved to Cambridge, and eventually amalgamated with Westminster College, Cambridge, when the Congregational Church joined the Presbyterians as the United Reformed Church.

The fate of the chapels was not dissimilar. Lady Huntingdon issued her fifteen articles, a revision of the order of service of the Book of Common Prayer. The control of the chapels after 1791 was initially in the hands of her friend Lady Anne Erskine who attempted to continue the authoritarian tradition of the foundress. This state of affairs was terminated early in the nineteenth century, and the "connexion" was thereafter administered by trustees.

Lady Huntingdon was very much a creature of her time. She believed in the correctness of the social order of the day. She died in London on 17 June 1791, in the same year as John Wesley. She was to be buried in the same tomb as her husband in the parish church at Ashby-de-la-Zouch. Perhaps the best summation of her can be found in the writings of George Whitfield, who noted on an occasion when she was ill that prayers were said for her recovery and "thousands joined in the singing of the following verses for her Ladyship":

> Gladly we join to pray for those
> Who rich with worldly honours shine,
> Who dare to own a Saviour's cause,
> And in that hated cause to join;
> Yes we would praise those that a few
> Love thee though rich and noble too.
>
> Uphold this star in thy right hand –
> Crown her endeavours with success,
> Among the great ones may she stand
> A witness to thy righteousness,

> Till many nobles join thy train
> And triumph in the Lamb that's slain.

Truly she could account herself as a lady of quality who "had found at the Cross and Mercy seat the happiness . . . [she] had sought in the world." She gained this spiritual satisfaction through conviction, but also because she was entirely able to follow her own whims. Being wealthy and a peeress she could act in an authoritarian fashion. Lesser mortals were expected to bow the knew; and when they did so they were treated in a gracious fashion, but if they were obdurate or independent they could be expelled from the Garden of Eden devised by Selina Huntingdon. She was the first English woman to establish by her own efforts a successful and independent church. She overrode all opposition in creating the viable and successful "Countess of Huntingdon Connexion".

Ann Lee

Revivalist movements of various kinds have been aspects of Christianity almost from the beginning. "The Great Awakening" in America and the Methodist revival in England were part of this tradition. So too were the so-called French Prophets and the Quakers. Thus, the Shakers were not necessarily unusually unique.

The foundress of the Shakers, Ann Lee, was born on 29 February 1736. She was one of eight children. Her parents were of little consequence, but according to hearsay she seems to have had more affluent relations in London. However, the latter only played a very minor role in her life. Curiously, and particularly for that day and age, she was not baptised until she was six years old; the reason for dereliction on the part of her parents is not known.

Ann Lee presumably never went to school, and surviving evidence would indicate that she was only semi-illiterate at best. She went to work in a factory at the age of sixteen; four years later she became a cook in some sort of infirmary or asylum for the poor and the insane.

Like many of her contemporaries in similar social circumstances she found the Church of England austere and remote. In 1758 she became interested in the teachings of James and Jane Wardley. The couple were Quakers of sorts, but a decade earlier had become adherents of a religious movement that was an off-shoot of the French Prophets. This group became known as the Shaking Quakers, because of its manifestations of possession by the Holy Spirit. These took the form of physical activity – twitching, jumping and dancing – and also speaking in tongues in unintelligible dialects. There was also a sort of hymn singing, wordless humming to popular tunes.

Initially, Ann Lee was just one of the sect inspired and directed by the Wardleys, not being influential in any particular fashion. Early in 1762 she married Abraham Standerin who was a blacksmith. The couple were to have four children, all of whom died in infancy. These deaths may well have contributed to her ultimate insistence upon celibacy, and her rejection of traditional marriage. She seems to have taken the stance that the loss of her children was a sign of divine displeasure, apparently becoming convinced that in rejecting all sexual advances by her husband she could achieve salvation. In due course she was to believe that celibacy was the requirement for others to attain the same goal.

Gradually she assumed a more public and prominent role. She began to proclaim a mystical theology, and was seen as the central figure of the Shaking Quakers. The local authorities did not hold the sect in high regard as being disorderly and against the accepted social order. Ann Lee was arrested, and during her imprisonment an attempt was made to starve her to death. She was miraculously preserved by the activity of a follower who ingeniously inserted a clay pipe in the keyhole of her cell, and provided her with liquid sustenance of wine and milk. When she was accused of blasphemy her opponents were confounded when she began speaking in seventy-two languages. Later she was charged with witchcraft being seemingly unaffected by beatings, starvations and being thrown from an upper window of the prison. In the summer of 1772 she was found guilty of disreputable behaviour on the Sabbath, and a year later imprisoned for disrupting the services in her local parish church.

While in prison Ann Lee had her first major vision; she was made aware of how mankind was separated from God after the Fall and that she was to be the agent of the new message. In later years she was seen by her followers as Christ's special messenger, whose her preachings were not her own words but those of Christ himself. After this mystical experience she regarded Christ as her spiritual husband, and would say of herself, "I am Ann the Word!" Once free from gaol she assumed publicly the position formerly held by Jane Wardley, and was accepted as the leader of the Shaking Quakers. In a sense Jane Wardley had been to Ann Lee what John the Baptist was to Jesus Christ. The Wardleys seem not to have resented the diminution of their role because they accepted her special attributes and the truth of her revelations.

She declared that all forms of mortal distress were the consequences of human carnality. Sexual activity was the principal source of damnation. The Shaking Quaker beliefs were summarised as follows. Firstly, that God's presence was always with them and it took such forms as ecstasy, dance, preaching and mystic healing. A later hymn cogently gave text to these feelings:

> We love to dance, we love to sing
> We love to taste the living spirit
> We love to feel our union flow
> While round and round and round we go.

Secondly, that confession was a requirement, a confession made to an elder of sinful acts in thought, word and deed; thirdly, compulsory celibacy permanent and total. Initially there was no form of organised worship, everything was spontaneous. It was noted by their detractors that they were often nearly naked, and that their dancing could be compared with contortions of those under torture. Ann Lee personally designated certain individuals who could receive the confessions of the faithful and thereafter forgive sin. Her visions she put into words so that others might share in her mystical experiences.

While initially Ann Lee's new-found role seems to have gone unchallenged, gradually her restrictions and prohibitions were deemed by some to be unduly demanding. By 1773 there was to be a schism. There was to be the more conservative faction in which the Wardleys resumed a leading role and the more radical one headed by Ann Lee. It was to be the latter faction who were to move to the New World.

The proposal to emigrate did not originate with Ann Lee but with James Whittaker, an adherent who had a vision of the church established in America. The vision was that of a great tree, and it represented the church in all of its glory. Relating the vision to Ann Lee, Whittaker asked for her support. She approved of the project and a decision was taken in favour. A few select persons were to make the journey; the more affluent subsidised the remainder. Abraham Standerin, the husband of Ann Lee, was to be one of the party. A wealthier member, John Hocknall, arranged for nine individuals to sail from Liverpool to New York.

They left on 10 May 1774 on the *Mariah*. The trans-Atlantic crossing was uncomfortable; there were gales and the sea was very rough. Added to these discomforts the vessel sprang a leak, and all had to man the pumps. For a time it seemed as if the *Mariah* would founder. However, according to legend, Ann Lee observed to the harassed captain that all was not lost for she had seen the angel of God who promised safe passage. At this juncture, it was said that a huge wave lashed against the ship and pushed back the loose plank through which the water was entering the hold, thereafter the vessel was totally sea-worthy.

The trip took three months; they landed on 6 August, a Sunday. Ann Lee and her party called upon the household of an individual with whom they had no personal acquaintance, and informed the residents that God had commanded that she and her friends should be provided with a home by these strangers. The householders seemingly were not overly surprised by the visitors, and provided the strangers with generous hospitality. They were to employ Ann Lee as a domestic servant, and her husband, the blacksmith, had a job in their benefactor's business.

In due course all of the travellers found jobs of sorts and assumed a fairly independent existence. However, it was always understood that in due course a proper community would be established. After making enquiries, possibly from a local Quaker meeting, John Hocknall and James Whittaker left New York and went to Albany. Near this town they managed to rent a sizeable tract from the Van Rensalaer estate. The advantage of this site was that the Hudson River provided easy access. John Hocknall was to declare that it was God himself who had guided him to the site which was called Niskeyuna.

Hocknall and Whittaker returned to New York, and, shortly thereafter the former went back to England. After a stay of brief duration he and his family, accompanied by John Parrington, a man of some considerable wealth, re-crossed the Atlantic. During their absence Ann Lee continued much as before. She and her husband now parted company completely; he left her for a life of alcohol and debauchery; she had very little money and was periodically cut off from her friends almost totally.

However, with Hocknall's re-appearance things improved considerably. The group, now joined by the new arrivals, moved to Niskeyuna. Here they erected a loghouse and a building to house visitors and to provide a place for the holding of religious services. Their neighbours regarded them with some caution, and, especially after the outbreak of the American War of Independence, they were deemed to be potential loyalists. The community was probably sustained by Revelation 12:1: Ann Lee was undoubtedly the "woman clothed with the sun, with the moon under her feet and on her head a crown of twelve stars". She never wavered in her belief of her mission; she encouraged the community by asserting that God would never have brought them to the New World if He had not intended for them to succeed. William Lee, her devoted brother, had occasional doubts, but these were overcome by her fortitude. She continued to believe that legions of potential converts were at hand. In the spring of 1779 she ordained that extra foodstuff should be collected because, as she observed, "we shall have company enough before another year comes about to consume it all". As it transpired she was to be quite correct.

The hoped-for mass conversion was to be the result of a revival in June 1779 in New Lebanon, New York and Hancock, Massachusetts. It was the consequence of New Light Baptist preaching, and the effects were not dissimilar to those experienced at Shaker meetings. Some months later, two individuals, who had not yet found a satisfactory route to salvation, made their way to Niskeyuna. When they arrived they were given a hearty welcome, and were told the following things: firstly, that Christ had already made his reappearance; secondly, that the day of resurrection for each person depended upon the confession of sin and thereby being personally saved; thirdly, upon entering the life of the spirit "the world" as previously known ceased to exist; and finally the committed declared that they were the people who had turned the world upside down.

Astonished by what they had been told, and impressed by the sincerity of their hosts, the two visitors returned home, and gave an account of what they had learned. Calvin Harlow, a friend and associate of the previous visitors, himself made an investigation. He wanted essentially to enquire how the leader Ann Lee had the temerity to speak in church in defiance of the express prohibition of St Paul in 1 Corinthians 14, verses 34 and 35.

Her response to his query was perhaps the most profound interpretation of her position. Man is in God's image, she said; nature required both men and women to procreate. Within the proper order of being man is first and woman second, the latter is subject to the former and the children subject to both. To the family he is the father and she the mother – Mother was capitalised in her written remarks. When only she remains, the "Mother" is the governing individual. "So" she "is the family of Christ." These comments answered his query. Once he accepted the premise that she had Christ's authority all else fell into place. Calvin Harlow was inspired by her charisma and was converted. He returned to New Lebanon, and persuaded his intimate friends that they should accompany him to see Ann Lee and her associates.

This third meeting had momentous consequences. The visitors saw and believed. They accepted that celibacy was a requisite for salvation without which they could not share in resurrection, and they agreed that while the cross was heavy so was the cross of Calvary. They publicly confessed, and were received into the community. One of them, Joseph Meacham, was to be defined by Mother Ann as her first-born son who would play a special role following her demise.

Soon after these events there occurred the famous "Dark Day". On that mid-May day, the sun did not shine, the sky turned yellow and blood red, the world was clothed in darkness – candles were required at noon. The people began to wonder if this was a portent of the prophecy of St John. On the contrary, Ann Lee and her followers were convinced that this was the sign that they were to go and preach their message and convert the unbelievers.

The newly converted all more or less said the same thing. For example, one noted, "I quick found out which balanced my soul... Obedience to Mother was my salvation and promise of eternal life." They all confessed their sins, acknowledging that "lust" was the great sin. Hell was to be the torture chamber for sexual offenders. Ann Lee not only abhorred heterosexual relationships, but homosexual ones as well. Masturbation and bestiality she regarded as vile indeed.

Doctrine as such was not overly specific; Relevation in particular was the inspired text. The services were much as they had been in Manchester. The position of Mother Ann was all-important:

> What a loving tender Mother
> We have in this Gospel Day,
> And if we are subject to her,
> We shall never go astray.
> She is our kind mediator,
> And has taught us what to do,
> She has ever been our Saviour,
> And tender Parent too.

At this juncture, and really until the demise of Mother Ann Lee herself, the so-called English group provided the leadership. It was only later that the American converts took charge and in the process really made the Shakers into a formalised body. It should be emphasised that Ann Lee, her brother William Lee, James Whittaker and John Hocknall had an almost uncanny power in reaching out to the potential convert. The latter was made to feel a very special being with the knowledge that in believing one would be saved.

Mother Ann not only preached salvation but also emphasised the importance of work. "Do all your work", she asserted, "as though you had a thousand years to live and as you would if you knew you must die tomorrow." Tidiness, order and diligence were expected. Personal adornments, self-indulgence and gluttony were all proscribed. Charity and hospitality were praiseworthy attributes. Dogs and cats were not to be objects of affection and the keeping of animals as pets was forbidden. In a sense it could be said that Ann Lee was reiterating the virtues of the first American colonists, nursed as they were in Puritan doctrine.

It must be observed that there were critics. Reports circulated that in order for the members to show directly that they were free of the sins of the flesh, on occasion they danced in the nude. This may have occurred at Niskeyuna but only very rarely. Also there were some who thought that the singing and dancing were the consequence of drunkenness. Actually, though, for their time the Shakers were generally abstemious.

The Shakers had not only an adherence to celibacy, but also to pacifism. The latter came from their original Quaker roots. In the summer of 1780 reports reached certain New York patriots that the Shakers were secret supporters of the British cause. The authorities ordered the arrest of Mother Ann and several others. An apostate, Valentine Rathbone, denounced them, but there was no real proof of the charges, and they were released after being imprisoned for about six months. Once freed the prisoners felt vindicated in their beliefs and embarked on renewed missionary activity.

They visited various communities preaching and evangelising; they were not always made welcome but they persevered. One town in Massachusetts was singled out for special attention. It was called Harvard. It had been the headquarters of an earlier revivalist named Shadrack Ireland. Some of his ideas were not too dissimilar to those preached by Mother Ann, including an advocacy of celibacy. This was to be abandoned when Ireland, claiming to be the second Messiah, took a wife. He built the so-called "Square House" for his headquarters. He did not inhabit it for long, dying soon after he took up residence.

Ann Lee asserted that Ireland earlier had been a true prophet, but that he had fallen from grace, and he was now in hell. This she knew true as she had seen him in a vision, and it was her duty to rescue those who had been deceived by him. She acquired his former headquarters and based her mission in it. There were difficulties. Some of Ireland's former adherents rejected Mother Ann's efforts and there was latent local hostility generally because of the continued suspicions about their political loyalties. Nevertheless they continued to preach their message. Some of the converts were known to have been convinced that Mother Ann and her intimate circle were immortal. She denied that such was the case. To be sure when the millennium came all true believers would be transformed into pure Spirit but until that day arrived death was not to be avoided.

By now there was a gradual development of community living. This, of course, was essential if the principle of celibacy were to be maintained. Manual labour was important to provide an economic basis.

One more brush with the law ensued. In the spring of 1783 Ann Lee and her closest followers were arrested for blasphemy, fined twenty dollars, and ordered to be expelled from Massachusetts. Three American disciples refused to leave and were gaoled. The others accepted the decision, albeit reluctantly, and went to New York and Niskeyuna.

The more practical members of the community, such as James Whittaker, had come to the conclusion that a more realistic and orderly direction was needed. They did not doubt that Ann Lee was inspired and that she and her brother William Lee advocated a strong sense of freedom, and used their spiritual gifts for the benefit of all. Whittaker was to wish for structure in all aspects, worship and in life. There were rumblings of discord, for William Lee seems to have believed that he was to be his sister's destined successor. He resented openly the authority presumed by Whittaker. The problem never had to be settled because William Lee predeceased his sister, dying in July 1784 aged forty-four.

It appears that Ann Lee herself began to decline in health shortly thereafter. The previous four busy and hectic years had left her weary and exhausted, and the demise of her brother at a relatively young age much depressed her. For a decade and a half she had been experiencing visions, preaching and converting. Emotionally she was totally at an end, and she was to die on 8 September 1784. Just prior to her demise she is reported to have said, "I see Brother William coming in a golden chariot to take me home." Her funeral attracted both the curious and the committed.

Her unexpected death caused a minor crisis. The millennium was at hand but without the leader. Having denied her own immortality, she was now with God and had risen to heaven. The Holy Spirit which had expressed itself through Mother Ann was not removed, but in itself re-directed. James Whittaker, her "beloved son", had been obviously her designated successor. She, however, remained the central figure, the special person mentioned by St John in Revelation. She was still clothed with the sun and was "Everywhere present as God Himself is."

The Shaker movement was to have in a sense a new beginning. It was to become more regulated and less spontaneous in expression. By 1806 the remarks of Ann Lee and her immediate successor were to appear as *The Testimony of Christ's Second Appearing*. There was a spiritual life to be attained by repentance and confession, an acceptance of celibacy, a life apart from the world, a unified organisation with a community of interests living in harmony and equality. The United Society of Believers in Christ's Second Appearing, the official name of the Shakers, was to be one of the most successful religious movements of the nineteenth century in the United States. The communities that were established were to be models of social order and discipline. Inevitably because of the insistence of celibacy and changing social mores, the Shakers as an entity vanished, only the physical artefacts remain.

One final note. Ann Lee's particular influence was in a sense re-established in 1837. Three girls at Niskeyuna were seen to be possessed by some special force. After consultation the elders decided they were imbued with the Holy Spirit. The girls said they had messages from Ann Lee, and two other early adherents, Lucy Wright and Joseph Meacham. The messages inspired new songs and forms of worship.

> At Manchester in England
> This blessed fire began
> And like a flame in stubble,
> From house to house it ran.
> A few at first received it,
> And did the lusts forsake;
> And soon their inward power
> Brought on a mighty Shake.

This revival was to be known as "Mother Ann's Work". It was a rededication of the simplicity of early days. In a sense the Shakers can be said to have presented a form of sacred theatre. It was ordered and directed, not haphazard and anarchic. Ann Lee had created a new sort of church almost solely through her own firm belief in her special powers. Her followers were to be certain that she had shown the world the one true way to salvation.

Joanna Southcott

Millenarianism has been part of the Christian world from very early days. Preachers have been prophesying the coming of the millennium and with it the return of Christ. Orthodoxy has tended to reject these beliefs and prognostications, and to regard these so-called prophets as dangerous radicals, as heretics or as lunatics. But the proponents of millenarianism often attract adherents, and such was to be the case of Joanna Southcott. In her case contemporary success was quite astounding; perhaps rather more so because as she herself observed, "This is a New Thing Amongst mankind, for a woman to be the Greatest Prophet that ever came into the world to bring out of darkness thy marvellous light and make every crooked path straight before you, and bring every mountain to a plain, and all dark sayings shall be brought to light." In addition to these pronouncements on herself and her mission, she also declared that she was to release Eve from being the agent of the Fall as was the accepted interpretation of scripture.

Joanna Southcott was born in late April in the year 1750. Her father was a moderately successful farmer, but he was to experience financial difficulties and was to become impoverished. The Southcotts were a pious family requiring their children to read the bible on a daily basis and to attend the services at their local parish church each and every Sunday. Joanna Southcott's mother was assiduous in instructing her children to be constantly aware of the wiles of Satan, and the hope, after repentance, of eternal salvation.

Another considerable influence on her was an elderly great-aunt. The latter apparently wrote a number of poems, some meditative prose and a few hymns. Her literary remains were read assiduously by her great-niece who found the sentiments expressed exceedingly consolatory in times of distress and personal unhappiness.

Joanna Southcott had little formal education; she could read and write, but her orthography was virtually illegible and her spelling often highly original. Later in life she tended to dictate her letters and her prophecies, and, when this was not possible, she seems to have instructed members of her circle to learn how to decipher her difficult handwriting. In her younger days she was regarded as an attractive woman. She did not lack for admirers, and several youthful swains proposed marriage. For various reasons, none very good, she rejected them all. It may well be that she did not envisage herself in a domestic and maternal role. Perhaps also, her social aspirations were higher than that enjoyed by a mere farmer's wife. However, at least two of her suitors were men of some wealth and enjoying moderately genteel social pretensions.

When she was forty-two years of age the so-called "Spirit" came into her life. It apparently occurred at about the time of her mother's death, and when she felt particularly depressed and in need of consolation. The "Spirit" took the form on occasion of a handsome youth whom she was to describe as being beautiful with a wonderful white skin. On the occasions that the "Spirit" shared her bed he was to caress and kiss her. In a very real sense the "Spirit" took on an erotic nature. "All of a sudden the Spirit entered me with such power and fury that my senses [were] lost . . . I felt as though I could walk on air at the time the Spirit was in me. . . ." She felt destined to become an intermediary with God through the "Spirit". Moreover, she was the "woman clothed with the sun, the moon under her feet and on her head a crown of twelve stars" (Revelation XII) and to give "birth to a son. . . . Who is to rule all the nations with a rod of iron!"

The idea or concept of the "Spirit" was not unusual in rural England in the eighteenth century. The local population regarded fairies, hobgoblins and wood nymphs as part of the world about them. They were special messengers from God directed towards prophecy and which manifested themselves in visions or dreams. If the messages were to be disregarded, and they were generally instructive, disaster would ensue. Joanna Southcott herself was to say, "I was informed I should be showed in dreams how things in the Nature came on." In other words she was convinced that she was given the mantle of the prophet. She did not see her powers as a form of witchcraft in the accepted sense. To her witchcraft was essentially evil in nature, and practised by wicked people under the influence of Satan. She herself was certain that the "Spirit" was from God.

Joanna Southcott believed that she had, through the "Spirit", the power to foretell events prior to their happening. She had no doubts that the failed harvests of 1799 and 1800 were the direct consequence of the local population not taking her seriously. "Her predictions were loud and frequent – full of comfort to her own subjects, dreadful denunciations to the rebellious creatures", as she was to write, "that did not acknowledge her sovereignty and trust to her prescience."

The Bishop of Exeter was of those who ignored her, and consequently she confidently predicted his imminent death – which shortly after ensued. It was hardly surprising that people feared her powers.

Astrology *per se* she disliked; the Bible and the "Spirit" were the only true prognosticators. Astrology she thought was just a means to deceive the naïve. However, there were caveats. Satan lived in the moon; planets had some influence although precisely how was uncertain. Comets were the harbingers of events that could affect all mankind. Her "Spirit" on occasion said of a comet, "I now tell thee that it is a sign of much greater events than have ever yet taken place."

Joanna Southcott might have remained almost totally obscure or at best only a regional figure had it not been for her desire to publish a pamphlet entitled *The Strange Effects of Faith*. This pamphlet, which appeared in 1801, contained the initial messages from the "Spirit". The contents were varied, some dealing only with everyday life and some with predictions for the future. Over the years she was to publish some 65 books and pamphlets. More of her writings were still unpublished when she died.

With respect to these writings, she declared they were the work of the "Spirit" very like the "Masters" and Madame Blavatsky or the automatic writing experienced by William Butler Yeats. She observed, "I know nothing and without the Spirit I can do nothing. . . . Every man that says my writings are my own invention . . . believes a lie, the truth is not in him who believes my writings are from myself."

The messages came to her at irregular intervals and often at great speed. This meant that for much of the time she had to be in the company of her amanuensis, perhaps a good thing since her writing is almost illegible. She argued that she frequently did not understand the full impact of the "Spirit's" communications. Generally speaking, however, despite the complexity of some of the ideas the language used was straightforward and plain, designed to instruct the ordinary individual. The messages from the "Spirit" took various forms, prose narrative, doggerel verse and aphorisms. While convinced that she wrote at God's command at the same time she often expressed herself as wishing not to be completely the creature of the "Spirit".

Very early she felt that she was not an isolated prophet, but part of a larger community sharing ideas. Her contemporaries frequently assumed that she emerged out of the Methodist movement and like those who were actively part of it that she was an "enthusiast". Robert Southey, the poet, actually dubbed her as a "Methodist prophetess".

Because she essentially associated herself with the lower classes she believed the Methodists would be her strongest supporters. This was not to be the case. In particular, the Calvinistic branch of the movement – Lady Huntingdon's Connection – she felt was most abhorrent. She opposed the idea of the elect as it lacked true Christian charity. Indeed, she was essentially an Arminian. She had become closely involved with the Methodists early in her experience with the "Spirit" asserting that it had ordered her to do so. Indeed, the "Spirit" seems to have insisted she associate with the Methodists even when she was far from happy with them. The "Spirit" declared that it did so to test her fortitude, only relenting after some time declaring to her, "Thou shall prophesy in my name, and I will bear thee witness."

Despite this association with the Methodists she continued to regard herself as an Anglican, and publicly said that she was a member of the Established Church. Although allowing the setting up of chapels devoted to her teachings, she did not want her followers to break with the Church of England. She had no wish to found a separate denomination but something parallel to the traditional parish church. Her principal desire was for the Church of England to be associated with her perceived mission to bring the country to God. Generally speaking her hopes were not to be realised; the majority of the episcopate and clergy rebuffed her efforts at a closer union. On one occasion she asked that a sort of synod be set up consisting of twenty-four clerics and twenty-four of her supporters but nothing came of it.

The ultra orthodox regarded her as "that woman Jezebel who calls herself a prophet and is teaching and beguiling..." (Revelation II:20). One said of her that she was but "An untutored female" and that she was incapable of "the conveyance of divine truth". As a consequence of these rejections, she predicted that society would suffer with bad harvests, defeat in the war with France and some form of divine displeasure on the Anglican establishment. She really wanted a thoroughly ecumenical national church to encompass all social classes. She did not favour schism, but was essentially a theological egalitarian. Macaulay, the historian, observed that if she had been a Roman Catholic she might well have founded an order of Discalced Carmelites. The intelligentsia, when they thought about her at all, considered her fraudulent and a mountebank whose sole aim was to delude the poor.

Despite her initial intention to the contrary, those who supported her beliefs became increasingly radical. This was in part the consequence of the general economic malaise in the first years of the nineteenth century. There were riots in Exeter and elsewhere and with the general impoverishment of the population, life for many was exceedingly harsh. Joanna Southcott offered the prospect of a happier and better existence. She announced that the Second Coming of Christ was relatively imminent, and, while mankind might presently be poor, starving and homeless, in the new millennium they would be happy and prosperous.

The continued economic and agricultural tribulations, and the prospect of a French invasion, induced more to believe in her mission. She left "the West Country" and took up residence in London where she was to live with Jane Townley, a woman of some private means, who, with her maid, Ann Underwood, was to provide her with a proper home until her death. She made a number of tours to spread her message and was amazingly successful. Her followers were required to take an oath, the text of which had been dictated by the "Spirit". "Wilt thou swear to Him that liveth – thou wilt obey in all things my strict commands to thee – and it is not all the Powers of Earth and Hell shall make thee turn to the right or to the left, but my command the living Lord of Heaven and Earth thou wilt obey". The converted accordingly took the oath as prescribed by the "Spirit", and in so doing since Joanna Southcott was the "Spirit's" emissary were taking an oath of obedience to her.

The saved were so indicated by being "sealed", that is to say they received a special document which indicated that the named individual had received a special blessing. There was a short text and "the seal" bore Joanna Southcott's signature. The "Scaled", for example, would survive any French invasion, the unbelievers would die in the streets. The "Sealed" signed or made their mark indicating that they had accepted the message of the prophetess. There was a virtual "run" on seals, and thousands clamoured to obtain one. It should be noted that at no time was any charge made for "the seal". The "seals" became like medieval relics, and were often buried with the deceased. The "sealed" who died before Christ's coming were thereby provided with a sort of passport to direct salvation at the latter date.

As a consequence of sealing, missionary tours and the establishment of chapels, many people became associated with the prophetess. It has been reckoned that at one time there may have been some two million individuals connected with her in one way or another. Her writings had a vast readership and it has been estimated that her pamphlet, *A Word to the Wise*, between 1801 when it appeared and 1816 two years after her death, over 100,000 copies were printed. All of her writings were to run into several editions.

The membership could be divided two to one in favour of women. The latter, as a consequence of Joanna Southcott's preachings, were blameless in the expulsion from Eden, and in a sense Eve was forgiven the apple. Christ was the divine spouse, and He would give His protection to all women and in particular to those who were unmarried. In a very real sense she liberated her own sex from a sense of guilt. The very success of the movement inevitably required some proper organisation. There were chapels with designated preachers, the latter were ultimately licensed to preach under the Toleration Act as members of a Protestant dissenting sect. This state of affairs resulted only when she was convinced the Church of England was not to be "reformed" according to her wishes and beliefs.

In her chapels in due course there was an order of service with hymns generally of a cheerful nature, the text often being the poetical effusions of the "Spirit". There was a sermon in which the preacher expounded the writings of Joanna Southcott for the congregation. There was also a sort of communion, the ritual requiring wine to be poured into a cup from which the women present would partake initially since Christ was coming to remove the guilt imposed on them through "the Fall". Each participant male and female repeated, "May I drink deep into the Spirit of Christ and may His blood cleanse me from all sin." On occasion the service was concluded with all present rising to their feet and with arms in the air saying three times in unison, "The will of the Lord be done, come Lord Jesus, O come quickly."

The "Sealed" were required to wear sober dress but nothing extreme. While the "Sealed" had a special place in the divine plan, they were not an "elect". All could share in the thousand years of God's reign and in the blessings that followed the coming of Christ. After which Satan will have been finally defeated, and there would be universal forgiveness for sinners and saints alike.

The principal tenet was that God's kingdom was at hand. She did not envisage the despoliation of the rich but rather that all should be prosperous. In the words of the "Spirit":

> And now let them like valiant soldiers stand
> And every foe shall bow before them all
> This is my Prophecies, I tell you all
> And true believers nothing have to fear.

Why did people accept her teachings so enthusiastically? Firstly because the mundane prophecies about the harvest, the weather and the like were persuasive and not infrequently correct, thereby indicating that she was not a fraud. Secondly, they sought a new religious authority, and through it all believers could find the answer. Thirdly, mystical experiences were often felt by ordinary people, and these acquired a sort of legitimacy through Joanna Southcott. Finally, the world according to her writings and prophetic utterances would ultimately be transformed, and with it total happiness for all would ensue.

Her success somewhat alarmed the authorities for her activities seemed to the casual observer to be dangerously radical. She was seen to be a female Thomas Paine with her conscious egalitarianism. Actually, she regarded Paine with much hostility and whose followers were not really concerned for the general good of society as a whole. She never proposed a levelling of all social orders. She did not encourage visionaries, seers and the like for she was always apprehensive that such enthusiasts might subvert the true mission and also attempt to wrest from her the position of leader. She was both fearful and contemptuous of opposition, hence the significance of the oath when a believer was "sealed".

Suddenly the believers were dumbfounded when, in late 1813, the "Spirit" informed her that when she was aged sixty-five she would bear a child. The infant was to be a son called Shiloh. How did this state of affairs come about? The reasons for it are very unclear. Her followers were not increasing in number and with nothing unusually adverse on the horizon why was the Kingdom of God not an immediate prospect? The sudden pregnancy promoted by the "Spirit" for the birth of Shiloh as Christ's proconsul would ensure the defeat of Satan and the millennium could not be far off.

Not surprisingly this announcement was received with some scepticism. However, a number of medical men who examined her externally seem to have been convinced of the truth of the pregnancy, and publicly announced they were certain that Joanna Southcott's "Spirit" had reported the truth. Some women admitted to her presence asserted they could feel the child moving in her belly. As the date for the birth of Shiloh approached – it was supposedly about the middle of October 1814 – the mother-to-be was showered with gifts for herself and the prospective infant. Many of the presents were costly and often given by the faithful who could ill-afford to spend their money on such things. Ultimately there were so many gifts that it had to be indicated that no more were wanted.

If the "Spirit" had astounded the Southcottians, by announcing the prophetess's pregnancy, it went even further. In order to guarantee the legal legitimacy of Shiloh, Joanna Southcott was ordered to marry.

The prospective groom was John Smith, a not particularly prepossessing person. The couple went through a form of matrimony in mid-November. It was agreed in advance that if no offspring, namely Shiloh, were born, the so-called marriage would be terminated. The public became increasingly avid for information, to satisfy popular curiosity a series of biographical pamphlets on the life of the prophetess were made available.

Soon after the wedding and with no sign of the anticipated infant, Joanna Southcott's own faith in the matter began to waiver. On the nineteenth of November she observed to her closest friends, "You have sometimes heard me say that I doubted my inspirations, but you would never let me despair, when I have been alone it has often appeared delusion," but when "communications come, I did not in the least doubt. Now it all appears delusion." It was a tragic verdict on her life and with it her abandonment by the "Spirit".

By late December it was evident that Joanna Southcott was dying. On Christmas Day her reported remarks were perhaps less tragic than those which she had uttered a month previously. She said, "I am not afraid to appear before my God, as I have done nothing but what I believed to be in true obedience to my Lord." She lapsed into a coma and expired on 27 December 1814. It was an auspicious day, the Peace of Ghent had just been signed, and the Anglo-American war was at an end. Perhaps this was the first sign of the foretold millennium.

Joanna Southcott's body was kept warm for four days to ensure that she was actually dead and not in a trance. There was a postmortem conducted thereafter, but to the medical practitioners of the day there was no obvious sign of the cause of her demise. It may well be that she died of cancer, very like Queen Mary Tudor. A false pregnancy could have been the result of cancer of the uterus. There was certainly no evidence of Shiloh. The first explanation was that the birth had somehow been postponed because of the attitude of the Anglican Church and, in particular, the episcopate's rejection of her mission. The second was that birth in the physical sense was never intended, that Shiloh would be recognised in himself as a prince destined to rule. Her funeral was a simple one, the service was that ordered by the Book of Common Prayer. In general it was poorly attended, particularly so for one who had been so influential. She was interred in the cemetery at St John's Wood in London.

Her death left her movement generally rudderless. A number of persons attempted to assume her mantle and to gather the "sealed" around them. The lack of a charismatic figure really meant that the Southcottian chapels declined in importance.

The famous box or boxes appear to have not been lost. Up to 1801 the prognostications were put into a sealed box on 31 December. The box was not to be opened except in the presence of twenty-four bishops. If her instructions concerning the opening were not followed, dire consequences would ensue.

The box passed into the possession of the Stuckey family. Through the efforts of Alice Seymour, various attempts were made to arrange for twenty-four bishops to attend the formal opening ceremony. Indeed, the Panacea Society in Bedford offered a large house with twenty-four bedrooms (and a bathroom) for them to stay in when they came to open the box. A "box" was opened in Westminster Hall in 1927 but without the requisite episcopal attendance. Little was found in the box; there were a few letters, some trifling aphorisms but no great collection of prophetic utterances, but it appears that this was the wrong box.

The Southcottian movement did not completely die out. in Chicago, USA, a branch had been established, which survived until 1922 when its leader was imprisoned for sexual crimes. Many British Israelites regard her as one of their founder figures. The Panacea Society, adhering to the teachings of Joanna Southcott, gained considerable fame for its apparent success in faith healing, and still retains its chapel and the house for the bishops. It also claims possession of the original box.

It should not be thought that Joanna Southcott's mission was a total failure. In her own day she brought hope to many of the poor. The prospect of an imminent Second Coming brightened their existence. Even if the promise of Revelation did not actually occur, over the century there was a general alleviation of the harshest conditions of life experienced by her chief followers.

Perhaps the Spirit should have the last word.

> And now let them like valiant Soldiers stand,
> And every foe shall now
> > Before them fall
>
> This is my prophetess, I tell you all
> And true believers nothing
> > Have no fear.

Barbara Juliana, Baroness De Krudener

Social class does not determine necessarily special religious sentiment nor for that matter does geography. The Baltic provinces of the Russian empire were relatively isolated from the essentially Slavic culture of the mass of the population. The denizens of Riga or Tallinen, for example, were generally Protestant rather than Russian Orthodox, and were somewhat Scandinavian in outlook, having formerly been governed from Stockholm rather than St Petersburg. They were often referred to as "Baltic Germans" rather than as Russians. Riga had cultural ties with Germany, and had been at one moment in its history a member of the Hanseatic League.

Barbara Juliana von Vietinghof was born in Riga in 1764. Her father was Otto Herman, the Baron von Vietinghof, and her mother, Anna Ulrike, was the Baroness von Munich. Both the maternal and paternal families were of aristocratic background; it should be observed also that the title baron was not generally given to a native Russian, but reserved either for distinguished foreigners such as the eminent British physician, Baron Dimsdale, or as a way of ennobling "Baltic German" grandees. The von Vietinghof family were wealthy with extensive country estates as well as a handsome and palatial residence in Riga. They were generally thought to be cultured with interests in the dramatic arts and music. In the country they had a private theatre for the production of plays and concerts.

Jean Jacques Rousseau's *Emile* had been published shortly before Barbara Juliana's birth, and while there is no proof that the von Vietinghofs had read the book, the ideas expressed in it were experienced by their five children. Not for them was a life of luxury; rather they were brought up in a simple and frugal manner. Added to this was a strong sense of Lutheran piety.

The rural estate at Kosse was a favoured residence. The place had a sort of melancholy rustic charm, and very early on Barbara Juliana was imbued with the agreeableness of her surroundings. The appeal of the rustic life was very much in harmony with the sentimentality of the day. It would appear too from later accounts that early in life she had a form of social conscience being much concerned for the welfare of the local peasantry.

When she was thirteen she and her parents went on an extended tour visiting Hamburg, Weimar, Amsterdam and Paris. The von Vietinghofs stayed for some months in the French capital enjoying all of the luxuries and charms of the city. Barbara Juliana recollected in later years that for her the best part of the sojourn was being taught to dance by the famous Madame Vestris. In due course the family returned to Courland, and life resumed its accustomed round in Riga and Kosse as before for the next few years.

By the time their daughter was eighteen her parents began to consider seriously the prospect of her marriage. In their world the prospective son-in-law would be chosen by them. In this instance, the individual finally selected was somewhat surprising. They encouraged Burchard von Krudener to approach their daughter as a prospective suitor. He was some twenty years her senior, had been married twice before, twice divorced, and he had a daughter only five years younger than his future wife. These seeming disadvantages were outweighed by his not inconsiderable wealth, his social position was impeccable – he too was of aristocratic lineage – and he already had a career of some importance, holding various diplomatic posts as a representative of the Tsar.

Von Krudener seems to have been a rather formal individual, not overly inclined to sentiment and generally intellectual and socially sophisticated. Juliana von Vietinghof – the Barbara seems to have been dropped during the sojourn in Paris – accepted her suitor's proposal in marriage for the obvious reasons. Under no circumstances could it be considered a love-match but in every way pre-eminently suitable to the social conventions of aristocratic families. The wedding took place in Courland in 1782, and the bride's father presented her with the estate at Kosse as an indication of the great affection he had for his favourite child. As the mistress of Kosse she was to have an augmented position in society and an adequate income solely under her own control for the rest of her life.

The newly married couple left Courland, and went to reside in Venice where the groom had been named Russian ambassador to the Republic. After leading an existence for the last few years of rural simplicity and relative unsophistication, life in Venice must have seemed almost magical. It was a great contrast to much of her previous experience, for Venice was worldly, elegant, gay and pleasure-loving. Her new home was in a magnificent palazzo and the entertainments given by the ambassadorial couple were, as expected, on a grand scale. Juliana von Krudener's only complaint it seems was that her husband spent too much of his day giving attention to business and not enough to the pleasures offered by the city.

After four years in Venice, von Krudener was named minister in Copenhagen. This was a posting of considerable importance because the Russian government kept the Kingdom of Denmark very much in thrall with the threat of reviving the claims of the Grand Duke Paul to his family estates of Holstein Goltorp. Juliana von Krudener and her stepdaughter, Sophie, did not immediately join the diplomatist in his position; rather the two women with a suitable entourage decided to make an Italian tour. They visited Parma, Modena, Tuscany and Naples. After the stylishness of Venice the Danish capital must have seemed very provincial to the two women when they finally arrived. The following year, 1787, a daughter, Juliette, was born. Life for Juliana von Krudener was agreeable enough, but without much charm and was essentially tedious. In the early spring of 1789, she decided to take her infant daughter to Paris. The ostensible reason for this plan was that the Danish winters were too harsh for the child. More probably the domestic life of the von Krudeners was in a state of collapse.

If Venice had been infinitely agreeable, then Paris in 1789 must have also seemed similar. The city was the centre of culture and of intellectual excitement. The revolution, which was to make such a radical change in society, had not yet occurred. In Paris Juliana dropped the "von" replacing it with the "de", and it was as Baroness de Krudener she was to be known thereafter in European society.

While in Paris she fell under the influence of Bernardin de St Pierre, a *litterateur* whose writings were not dissimilar to those of Rousseau. Her correspondence with him and with other friends reflected similar sentiments. The taking of the Bastille, the Tennis Court Oath and the like do not seem to have affected her daily life. In the autumn of 1789 she and her daughter went to Montpellier, and, some time in the next eighteen months she had a brief love affair with a handsome young officer named de Fregé. Conditions of life in France were becoming increasingly hazardous and upon the solicitations of her husband she agreed to return to Copenhagen. Almost immediately upon her arrival in the Danish capital she asked her husband for a divorce. It may well be that she hoped to marry Fregé. Von Krudener was disinclined to accede to her request, but as a sort of compromise he agreed to a formal separation. This put into effect, she went back to Riga.

While Copenhagen had seemed provincial after Venice, one can only assume that a sojourn in Riga after Paris must have been tedious indeed. Meanwhile von Krudener had been transferred to Berlin and he requested his wife and children to join him. They were to do so but not for a lengthy duration. Apparently she was incapable of settling anywhere, moving from place to place in an aimless fashion. Once again there was an attempt at a proper reconciliation but this too failed and a final and formal break ensued. It was at this juncture that her initial interest in religious matters began; she turned to the faith of her family as a sort of cure for her generally unsuccessful and unsatisfactory existence.

Leaving her children with their father but accompanied by her stepdaughter, Sophie, she went to live in Switzerland. A few months later they were joined by her daughter, Juliette. During her sojourn in Switzerland Juliana de Krudener paid a visit to Madame de Stael. Initially the encounter was an agreeable one but it soon became obvious that both women wanted to be at the centre of the stage. The problem was that the Chateau of Coppet in the Vaud was to Madame de Stael what Versailles had been to King Louis XIV. There could be no rival at court. The charms of life in Switzerland began to fade.

Paris, having recovered from the excesses of the Terror, became once more a possible place for Juliana de Krudener to live. Having now become a widow, she moved to the French capital in 1801, and she was determined to shine in literary and intellectual circles. Her first book was entitled *Pensées d'une dame étrangère*, modelled on La Rochefoucauld with aphorisms such as, "Life resembles the sea which owes its finest effect to storms." Far more successful was her novel *Valerie*, which attracted much attention. It was a sentimental tale, very over-written, but it had wide appeal and was translated into several European languages.

Tiring of her glamorous existence once again she returned to Riga and at the same time she began her idealisation of Tsar Alexander with his proposals for the moral improvement of society. His great aims are to be accomplished, she averred, through the will and hand of God. This new phase in her life was to be influenced by a chance meeting with a youthful member of the Moravian church or Unitas Fratrum. The consequence of this encounter was that she was to experience a real and total conversion.

The Unitas Fratrum was a Protestant body that arose from the Hussite reformation of the fifteenth century. After some three centuries of vicissitudes the surviving brethren settled themselves on the estate of Count Nicholas Zinzendorf. The settlement at Herrenhut was to emphasise a rich liturgical tradition with an emphasis on spiritual experience, the joyous nature of the believer, the specific significance of Holy Communion and the love feast to underscore Christian fellowship. Music was an important feature of their services.

The upshot of her conversion was that she replaced the world of the intellect with the world of belief. She wrote to a friend, "Pray, pray like a child! If you are not in this happy state, pray! Seek this divine grace which God always accords through the love of His Son. You will secure it, you will realise that man cannot be happy either in this world or the next without Jesus Christ, without the faith, that salvation comes only through them." This statement is very much in the Moravian spirit. With her newly acquired spirituality, she seeks to enhance it finding friends who are sympathetic. She made the acquaintance of Madame Blau, a religious fanatic overly imbued with a strong sense of mission, which she in turn conveyed to Juliana de Krudener.

In 1806 she moved to Konigsberg where she found a congenial circle. The conversations and ideas of her new acquaintances concentrated on the German mystics. Even Queen Louise of Prussia in semi-exile following her husband's defeat by Napoleon noted, "I have drawn nearer to God, my faith has become stronger and thus, in the midst of numberless humiliations and misfortunes I have never been without consolation and thus never truly unhappy." Juliana de Krudener could not have expressed her own sentiments more succinctly.

She was to become more imbued with the prophetic beliefs of the Unitas Fratrum following a meeting with the peasant prophet Adam Muller in 1807. His ideas as reinterpreted by her were to become the central theme of her preaching. Desiring to see a living Moravian community, she visited Herrenhut. She was much impressed with the ordered lives of the denizens, she admired the spiritual simplicity of the believers, and found the combination of faith and work edifying. She also seems to have accepted, at least on a first level, that titles, social class and wealth were inconsequential and that all individuals were brothers and sisters. One perhaps can be mildly cynical in suggesting that this was not the simple life of *Emile*, the utter guilelessness of Candide or Marie Antoinette playing the dairymaid. She, however, did not fail to expect deference due to her as a woman of rank, and she did not take up the simple life abjuring all creature comforts. It would also appear that she committed herself to the millenarian doctrine, the second immediate coming of Christ and the one thousand years of His reign.

Having been given a letter of introduction to Henrick Jung-Stilling, she sought him out and he, like Adam Muller, was to become a major influence in her life. Jung-Stilling was 67 years old, a Christian intellectual and a pensioner of the Grand Duke of Baden. His principal task in life as he saw it was to extend the Christian message in the widest sense. In so doing, he chose to regard all the ideas of the enlightenment as evil, the French Revolution as the result of the ruling classes accepting these iniquitous beliefs, and the violence that ensued was a form of just retribution. He thought that exponents of so-called liberal ideas should be confronted and refuted whenever possible. He was convinced that truly believing Christians would have no difficulties in demonstrating the evils that ensued from their false premises. He accepted the reality of the spirit world, and that spirits manifested themselves to true believers. According to him, each person had a guardian angel who took a very direct role in the life of that individual. Children were inherently good, and evil only entered their behaviour when they became adult. As a millenarian he thought the nineteenth century would be the new holy age, and that the Second Coming would occur in 1819. He advocated bible reading, good works, and he asserted that holiness came from within through the grace of God.

Juliana de Krudener was given a great welcome by Jung-Stilling when she finally met him in 1808. She revelled in his teachings and in the Christian practices of his domestic entourage. After being his guest for some time, she moved to Alsace where she went to stay with Frederick Fontaines. He, too, was a millenarian and was somewhat unorthodox in his theology. A woman named Marie Kummer was a member of his household; she was a prophetess of sorts and went into trances, experienced glossolalia and other forms of ecstasy. While in Fontaines's home Juliana de Krudener was introduced to the writings of Madame Guyon, thereby adding Quietism to her pietistic beliefs. Quietism reinforced many of her already accepted ideas of Christianity.

She and her companions moved to Wurtemberg. They must have seemed a very odd group of travellers indeed, Fontaines in black, Marie Kummer swathed in veils and Juliana de Krudener in blue and white. There is no record of how her daughters were dressed. King Frederick was hardly a gracious host, and immediately ordered them to leave the country. They returned to Baden where, for the moment, they were permitted to reside.

Under the influence of her friends, she seems to have accepted the concept of mystic death at which time all personal desires were subordinated so that a new life of the spirit might be engendered. Another idea, which also found her adherence, was mystic marriage in which a spiritual, not physical, union could occur for mutual prayer and meditation. Moreover, a mystic marriage between two persons might take place even if both parties were already married to others in legal wedlock. She seems to have entered into a mystic marriage with Fontaines, whom she called Hargott, which was a corruption of Herr Gott. This mystic marriage may have aided her on the road to salvation, but it brought her much criticism from her contemporaries who declined to believe the relationship was only spiritual. Moreover, it was thought to be particularly unseemly considering the vast gulf in their social status. Mindful of the hostility and the ostracism she was experiencing in Baden, she decided to return to Riga where she had estates and an establishment which would permit her to live as she chose.

While enjoying her rural retreat in Kosse, her mind was more and more concentrated on religious affairs. She came to the conclusion that despite the claims made by Roman Catholicism, its adherents saw only shadows, and that traditional Protestantism in general was not much better for it neglected what she regarded as the great mysteries. To resolve these difficulties it was essential "to turn to the Invisible Church in order to find Christians" because "the Lord has children everywhere". She assumed also a belief, which was heretical in all orthodox communions, namely, that any faithful believer not necessarily in holy orders could administer the sacrament. Her general philosophy of life might be summed up in an aphorism attributed to her: "Live from day to day, remembering that you are under the guidance of the most tender Love."

While life in the country had its attractions, she found local society not overly intellectually stimulating. She moved to Geneva where she had resided formerly. She had a salon of sorts, and also preached sermons which found little or no approbation from the local clerical establishments. Her theology was too *outré* and the Company of Pastors attempted to silence her. Things did not improve when a young man named Henri Empaytaz became an intimate friend. He was just the sort of youth to be influenced by Juliana de Krudener, just precisely the type of individual for whom the Company of Pastors felt the most concern. He was not a theologian *per se* although he had pretensions to be one. He seems to have been particularly adept at producing appropriate scriptural texts for her prayer meetings. Empaytaz was essentially a simple pietist who was convinced of the truth of her message. She was not an impostor, nor were her beliefs merely a pose, she had the virtues and vices of the enthusiast, the charms of an inspired individual.

During the last half dozen years, Juliana de Krudener had enjoyed the companionship of her stepdaughter and her daughter. The former, Sophie, had recently married the Marquis Ochondo; the latter, Juliette, was soon to marry Charles, Baron Berkheim. She had become acquainted with Roxana Stroudza, the secretary to the Tsarina Elizabeth, a princess of Baden and the wife of Tsar Alexander. The latter's secretary was incidentally the husband of Roxana Stroudza. The two women were frequent correspondents drawn together through a mutual admiration of Tsar Alexander. She noted in a letter,

> The Russian Emperor sets the example of devoutness by his profound piety and by the manner in which he ascribes credit to God for all of his victories. . . . The Russians teach the Name of all Names to the over-cultivated Germans and give praise to Christ.

The Tsar was destined to destroy the evil rationalism that had emerged from the French Revolution and to bring about a new and believing Christian era. She was convinced also that God would ensure that she would have the special pleasure of seeing the Tsar personally. She declared early in 1814, "I have tremendous things to say to him for I have suffered much on his account." Precisely what she meant by suffering in some special way for the Tsar is not entirely clear. All she had done on his behalf, it would appear, was by asserting rather frequently that God had special plans for the Tsar, and it was she who would be his mentor. Regarding the divine plans for the Tsar that such were "not unknown to the humble servant [herself presumably] who is to announce these things to him. . . . Pray for the elect of the Lord."

The Tsar was not unaware of her existence. Moreover, he was the ideal object of her special concerns. Educated by La Harpe in the true enlightenment tradition, he had rejected the rationalist teaching and had turned to the mysteries and beliefs of the Russian Orthodox Church. The death of his father, murdered by his friends, imbued in him a special sense of guilt. He became convinced that he had a higher mission than his fellow sovereigns, and this was to ensure the happiness of all and sundry in this world and the next.

Moreover, his private life was not overly happy; he and his wife were not compatible and, at best, they were only on the most formal terms. He had great affection for his mother and she influenced and reinforced his piety. Two other persons of his circle, the Metropolitan Philaret and Prince Galitzine, the head of the newly founded Russian Bible Society, played a similar role. Outward manifestations of his religiosity took the form on occasion of lying prostrate before the altar in the imperial chapel. Despite all of her efforts, Juliana de Krudener failed to receive a summons to the imperial court. She had to be content with an indirect communication with the Tsar by means of her correspondence with influential persons in St Petersburg.

Napoleon's escape from Elba early in 1815 and his restoration brought a grand coalition against him. Tsar Alexander was to be actively involved, being inspired in his cause by Daniel XI:15:

> Then the King of the north shall come and throw up siege works and take a well fortified city. And the forces of the south shall not stand, nor even his picked troops for these shall be no strength to resist.

On 4 June 1815 he arrived at Heilbroun not far from where Juliana de Krudener was residing. Earlier he had told Roxana Stroudza that he would give the former an audience but at some time in the future. Before the Tsar retired to his room, he gave instructions that he was not to be disturbed. During the course of the evening a lady arrived at his lodgings somewhat disguised with heavy veiling, and insisted on seeing the Russian monarch. Initially all her efforts were in vain, but she managed to speak to Prince Wolkonsky, an aide-de-camp, and implored him to use his good offices on her behalf. Somewhat reluctantly, he agreed and going to the Tsar he told him that Juliana de Krudener was in the guardroom craving an interview. The Tsar agreed. Apparently he had not known that she was in the neighbourhood. He was to say later,

> I received her at once and as though she had been able to read my soul she addressed me in hopeful and consoling words which calmed the agitation with which I had been overcome so long.

The Tsar and the mystic conversed for three hours. The gist of her message was that he was still a sinner, had not given himself to Jesus and that he had failed to say publicly, "God be merciful to me a sinner!" His failure to repent was the reason why he was so lacking in peace within himself. She concluded the interview with the remark, "Listen to the voice of a woman who has also been a great sinner but who has found pardon for all her sins at the foot of the Cross of Christ." Tsar Alexander, on hearing these prophetic words, burst into tears and begged her to come again to see him. She had found her most notable penitent; God had ensured her a role in the future universal kingdom. When the Tsar moved to Heidelberg she, her daughter and her son-in-law came to live nearby. Once more she had her usual *conversaziones,* and the Tsar was frequently present and heard to express phrases of pious sentimentality. His Egeria became more and more inclined to prophetic utterances, declaring that he must seek the heart of Jesus and that "the life of Christ" was to circulate morally through his "spiritual body". She said, "You [the Tsar] must be filled with the Divine Life. . . ."

Following the defeat of Napoleon at Waterloo, Tsar Alexander moved to Paris. There he was to be joined by Juliana de Krudener and her companions. Accompanied by Empaytaz they slowly made their way to the French capital. En route the caravanserai made frequent stops and sermons were preached at regular intervals. There were no difficulties encountered by the travellers as they had the patronage of the Tsar who had provided them with special Russian passports.

Once in Paris she found a residence close to her imperial convert, and he visited her frequently seeking her counsel and spiritual guidance. Benjamin Constant, the protégé of Madame de Stael, was also under her influence. He felt that every word had "a certain quality of eternity" and she seems also to have been capable of inducing floods of tears when he thought of his sinful nature. Even his rather worldly mistress, Madame Récamier, was impressed, and both were profoundly moved by her concern for their spiritual welfare. She had her detracts. Lord Castlereagh, the British Foreign Secretary, was generally unimpressed and he regarded her at best a fanatic and at worst a fraud.

Contrary to general opinion and despite the fact that Juliana de Krudener was to be called "Our Lady of the Holy Alliance", she had little political influence. She tried in vain to save General de la Bedoyere when he, like Marshal Ney, was found guilty of treason and sentenced to death. Tsar Alexander did, however, invite her to be present at the great military occasion on the Plain de Vertus when 150,000 Russian soldiers marched past in review. She was convinced that France had been defeated for impiety and regicide; the Russians, on the contrary, were loyal subjects and pious believers. She noted, "Here [on the Plains de Vertus] Jesus Christ was adored by the hero and by his beloved army, here the nations of the north prayed for the happiness of France."

Tsar Alexander owed something to her influence when he created the Holy Alliance. Politics and diplomacy were to be conducted "on the sublime truths contained in the eternal religion of Christ our Saviour". The name "Holy Alliance" probably came from the book of Daniel 11:30. Empaytaz asserted that the Tsar read the Bible every day, incidentally in a version in French not in Russian.

The mystic and her penitent met for the last time in France in October 1815. There was to be only one more personal encounter in the future. She was a curious melange of the radical and the reactionary, asserting as she did that rulers must be directed by Christian beliefs but at the same time avowing that royal powers were insignificant if not recognised as mere reflections of divine authority. A sovereign in himself was as nothing, he was only important as a divine instrument. Many of her contemporaries would have regarded such opinions as dangerous. Brief as her role in the great world had been, she had gained for herself a place in history.

Departing from Paris she moved to Switzerland where her son Paul served as the Russian representative to the Swiss Confederation. She resumed the holding of soirées dedicated to the promoting of her pietist theology and her millenarian beliefs. She seems to have wished to recapture the spiritual essence and enthusiasm of the early church and described herself as being "an old Catholic". Her numerous public addresses were delivered to sizeable congregations, but the clergy viewed her activities without enthusiasm.

She moved to Baden where she was not overly enthusiastically received by the local clergy. In part she engendered opposition because of the orthodox idea that a woman preacher was unscriptural. Her response to her critics was terse. She observed,

> It is said that women should not teach, but is not Our Lord the Master and does He not use whom He will, do not the Scriptures show us many women employed for the deliverance of the people?"

Further, she declared that all she was doing was spreading the Christian message in the best way she could. Some of her sentiments could be interpreted as potentially dangerous to the accepted social order as when she used religious language in preaching to the poor. She avowed that what she taught was the doctrine of the cross as in the Book of Revelation. She further said that she possessed special powers, and like the saints she could perform miracles. Her sincerity was obvious to all, but her eccentricity made her the object of critical commentary. To some her enthusiasm led the authorities to consider her deranged. She even went so far as to spell out her rules for prayer.

They were as follows: pray the first Monday of the month for missionaries to the heathen, prostrate oneself body and soul every Sunday, on Wednesday at five in the afternoon to ask divine protection for society, and thirdly pray every Saturday for a blessing in the forthcoming sermon on the Sunday following, and also for Livonans, citizens of Riga, Karlsruhe, Strasbourg, Basel, Geneva, among others. With ideas like this it is hardly surprising that the French authorities forbade her to enter the country being convinced that she was the leader of a secret society, and hence dangerous.

Juliana de Krudener and her companions – she called them "the Holy Mission" – some eighteen of them moved about Germany in a desultory manner. On occasion she was given a police escort to ensure that she did not establish herself permanently in any community. On reaching Erfurt she was without funds but the Grand Duchess of Saxe-Weimar, the sister of Tsar Alexander, paid her expenses. Generally speaking the various princely rulers attempted to silence her but with mixed success. She continued to regard the Tsar as "the elect of God", she praised the Holy Alliance and railed against rationalism. She attempted to impress even the most worldly with her convictions but at the same time being to them a misguided fanatic. Her correspondence with Tsar Alexander continued as in the past. The letters contained pious statements and admonitions, but the recipient did not invite her to St Petersburg. Her old friend, Roxana Stroudza, remarked that "His Majesty did not care" for another meeting.

Arriving in Frankfurt am Oder in January 1818, she and her travelling companions made preparations to stay for some months. While in the city she had her portrait painted, and the result was a very flattering likeness which she recognised to be the case but was pleasing to her having still some worldly sentiments. Leaving Frankfurt in the early spring she reached the Russian frontier where the authorities denied her admission. She appealed directly to the Tsar, requesting that the entire company be given admission to his empire. Tsar Alexander did not reply directly to her but sent a message to his agent in Mittau to whom he said that Juliana de Krudener was an emissary from God, not, as some had seen her, a tedious fanatic, and that no opposition should be shown to her preaching. Tsar Alexander noted in closing, "It is better to pray in any manner than not to pray at all". By the summer she was once more in Riga, and taking up residence in her country estate at Kosse she established a sort of religious community. Her tenants were more or less dragooned into being members along

Deviating Voices 93

with her travelling companions. There were frequent and compulsory church services, lengthy sermons and extemporaneous prayers. On occasion, she went into ecstasy inspired by the Holy Spirit, and delivered prophetic utterings. This state of affairs continued for three years. During this time she had occasionally written to Tsar Alexander but his replies were infrequent and generally indirect, being conveyed to her by mutual friends.

Leaving Kosse in the summer of 1821 she made her way to St Petersburg. En route she had generally been well received as it was recognised that she enjoyed the monarch's protection. Once settled in the imperial capital, as elsewhere, she maintained a salon of sorts where she preached and prophesied to her guests and distributed religious tracts. She felt somewhat bereft because the Tsar seemed so distant. She felt she had been "abandoned by the man who should have been one of the company of the Cross. . . . He had not a single flower for me, not even a cup of water." Finally he did write, apparently in a friendly manner, but firmly advised her against making any political comments whatsoever.

In the early autumn of 1821 she and the Tsar had what was to be their final meeting. What was discussed remains a mystery. She lingered in St Petersburg hoping that she would be called anew to the palace. This was not to be. Accepting her dismissal, she returned to Riga in the spring, and prior to her departure she sent the Tsar a farewell letter. He did not reply.

She took up her life in her religious community but shortly thereafter her private spiritual mentor, Pastor Kellner, died. She was much distressed feeling that one of her most trusted counsellors had left her unsupported in her endeavours. Nevertheless she remained at Kosse for two years.

In 1824 she was to make her last journey. Long convinced that good German peasants, hard-working and industrious, would make ideal settlers in the Caucasus, Juliana de Krudener aided by her son-in-law, Baron Berkheim, undertook to recruit such individuals to be colonists on the estate of her friend, Prince Galitzine. For reasons that are not entirely clear, she decided to accompany these Germans. As much of the journey was made by water, two boats were required. One was for the colonists, the other was for herself, her daughter, Juliette, and the Princess Galitzine. The ladies travelled in some style as their vessel was quite luxuriously fitted out; the other was not dissimilar for the use of the transport of cattle, horses and hogs.

During the lengthy journey she became unwell, but persisted in her intention to reach the Galitzine estate at Korais where she would reside over the winter. She hoped that her health would improve in the salubrious climate. She never did reach her final destination; forced to disembark at Korasu-Bazor she became increasingly frail. Aware that she had not long to live, she composed her own epitaph on her sixtieth birthday, 22 November 1824.

The good I have done will endure, the evil I have done (for how often have I taken God's command what proved to be only the fruits of my imagination and conceit) God in His mercy will blot out.

She died on Christmas Eve, 1824. She was buried in the Armenian cathedral at Korasu-Bazor. When report of her demise reached St Petersburg, it evoked little comment and no official recognition was given. Her friend, Galitzine, summed up her existence, "Such a life resembled shavings, when they are burned nothing remains but a tiny heap of ashes." Whatever else in her case there was a heap of ashes.

Curiously her early romantic novel ensured her reputation in the next decade. *Valerie* was reprinted in 1837 to considerable acclaim. She seemed to represent the enlightenment, the optimism and the liberal sentiments of the previous century. As for herself, she would have preferred to be remembered for a life of piety and evangelism rather than as a luminary of the Parisian salons. A modern author has written that her life was a tiny fragment

from the great manuscript of the past. Historical insight into any age is not entirely to be gained by contemplation of its leaders and the faded ribbon or the bit of tinsel may evoke former days more successfully than the full panoply of armour. Between the fragile Julie . . . and the broken old woman who died in the Crimea can be traced the footsteps of a life which explored most of the highways and many of the byways of an epoch.

Her voices had told her that she had a particular role to play, a particular mission to fulfil and, despite opposition and some derision, she had endeavoured to bring the Christian message to a wider scene. She had the great satisfaction that she, an erstwhile woman of the world, had eschewed its glitter and had brought one great penitent, Tsar Alexander, to fulfil his Christian destiny and with her to know God more fully and completely. This can surely be reckoned as no mean accomplishment.

Lydia Sellon

From the days of the dissolution of the English monasteries and nunneries in the 1530s, women within the Established Church tended to play only a passive role. There was no thought among either the clergy or the laity that it should be otherwise. Nobody could conceive of a function for women within the formal ecclesiastical establishment; it was only in the early years of the nineteenth century with a change coming about with the organisation of Anglican convents when there was a change. In general, however, such communities were regarded with suspicion as being signs of latent Roman Catholicism. Those involved with the establishment of sisterhoods had to face continued opposition and criticism. To be such an individual meant that one had not only to be imbued with the Holy Spirit, but also to be an intrepid and courageous person. Such was Priscilla Lydia Sellon. She was not, however, to be the first to establish a community. The earliest was Emma Langton who founded the Sisters of the Holy Cross, and the first professed nun in the Church of England since Mary Tudor's reign was Marian Rebecca Hughes who was dedicated to a religious life in 1841.

Priscilla Lydia Sellon was born on 21 March 1821 – the feast of St Benedict – the daughter of Richard Sellon, a naval officer. When Lydia was aged two her mother died leaving three children, Lydia, Anna and William. In due course Commander Sellon was to re-marry and to father a large family of eleven children. As was usual for that day for girls of the upper classes, Anna and Lydia had a governess. She was an austere individual who was a stern Presbyterian, and from her they were to learn the significance of the word duty. Lydia Sellon was from an early age independent minded. At no time could she ever have been considered a beauty but contemporaries report that she could be most charming and that in society she had an affable manner.

In 1846 she went to stay with John Chambers and his wife who lived in London. They were intimate friends of Edward Bouverie Pusey, a leading figure in the Oxford Movement. She made his acquaintance, and it was probably through him that she learned of the existence of the community of the Sisters of the Holy Cross.

The order, under the direction of Emma Langton was actively involved in nursing the sick, parish visiting and orphanages. The sisters lived under a rule that was a mélange of the precepts of St Francis de Sales and the Ursulines. They seem to have followed the traditional church hours – that is prime, lauds, tierce, etc. – and, except for the time in the choir and for a short period during the day, they kept silent. They had a habit of sorts, a plain black dress and a veil. When out of doors they substituted the veil for a bonnet and wore for warmth a shawl. While Lydia Sellon was generally impressed with the activities of the sisters when she visited their establishment at this time, she was not prepared to consider joining them. Moreover, her general state of health was assumed to be in a parlous condition, and her family thought she should spend the winter months in Madeira. Apparently acquiescing in this arrangement, she planned to leave England on New Year's Day 1848.

Fate intervened. Lydia Sellon happened by chance to read an article in *The Guardian*, a church newspaper, summarising an appeal made by Henry Phillpotts, the Bishop of Exeter. In his appeal he called for help in Devonport, one of the most densely populated towns in England, but one lacking churches, schools and hospitals. Lydia Sellon, perhaps attracted by the nautical traditions associated with the place, on impulse abandoned her plans. Devonport demanded her presence. She could not refuse the call made by the Bishop. With the approbation of her father, who seems to have put aside any misgiving she might have had with respect to her health and supported by her London friends, she volunteered to work in the slums.

After an initial survey of the scene, she reckoned there were some nine thousand young persons almost totally neglected, ill-educated and uncared for. Most had never even been christened, and many certainly had never attended a church service should a church even be part of the townscape. She decided that her first task would be to establish evening classes for boys most of whom worked in the dockyard in the day. Soon she had two hundred in regular attendance. She did not do all of the teaching herself, hiring a schoolmaster to assist her. There were the inevitable difficulties; the boys often behaved badly, there were frequent fights and general rowdiness, but she persevered. Aware that she could not reach all of those in need alone, she came to the conclusion that it was necessary to establish some sort of community to provide a broader base for her efforts. Her father highly approved of her accomplishments so far, and he was prepared to provide the funds to assist in bringing the new project into being.

Lydia Sellon sought out Bishop Phillpotts and proposed the creation of a proper order of sisters. After some cautious consideration he gave his approval. Lydia Sellon made another visit to the London community to ascertain if its aims and those of her own were complementary. She decided against joining the Sisters of the Holy Cross "but to form another [order] of which she should herself be Superior for work among the poor of Devonport." This would seem to imply that she was unwilling to submit herself to any authority that might be seen to diminish her efforts or to limit her freedom of action since Philpotts was not noted for laxity.

At this juncture she was joined by the most admirable of colleagues, namely, Catherine Chambers, the sister of her good friend, John Chambers. Catherine Chambers was to become Lydia Sellon's best friend and closest associate. She was evidently a woman of considerable beauty, but her good looks and social accomplishments seem to have masked a high degree of administrative competence. She was to become a sort of private secretary to her friend, thereby freeing the latter from many mundane tasks and allowing her to fulfil the goals of the sisterhood in a public fashion. Very soon the two women were joined by Ann Terrot who was a member of the London community. She brought with her a sense of what were the requisites of communal living, and an awareness of the difficulties that such an enterprise might expect to experience from the world at large.

The three women took a house in Clarence Place in Devonport in October 1848. While the night classes for the boys were not abandoned, they came to play a less important role. Others assumed responsibility for them, thus allowing Lydia Sellon and her two associates to turn their attention to what seemed more pressing needs. They decided to open a home for "the orphan daughters of British sailors and soldiers". Their aim was to rescue these girls from a life on the streets and with it the inevitable existence of prostitution. John Chambers did yeoman service in acting as the repository of the financial contributions required to maintain the orphanage. The results of the prospectus issued by Lydia Sellon were gratifying. Support came from Queen Adelaide, members of the aristocracy and parliament, military and naval officers – Commander Sellon was a major donor – and ordinary people. The upshot was that the orphanage came into existence very promptly. Also at the same time, on the feast day of St Simon and St Jude, the order of the Sisters of Mercy was formally established.

Having a sisterhood, it was essential that there should be a Rule. Lydia Sellon had not approved of the Rule of the London community; indeed, it was said that its strictness appalled her. She would institute a practical, albeit religious, set of regulations. Lydia Sellon was determined that unregulated asceticism was unrealistic; the physical well-being of the sisters was of a high priority in order that they could perform their allotted tasks in a sensible fashion. The rule defined the habit to be worn both in the house and outside. It was a plain and simple black woollen dress with a girdle, an ebony cross and a white cap, outdoors there was to be worn a heavy black shawl and a large black bonnet. Incidentally, the hair was cut short. Regulations were made as to the form of address, the lady superior being called "Dearest Mother" and the sisters as "Sister" followed by a Christian name. The specific object of the Sisters of Mercy was to educate and care for the daughters of sailors and soldiers, and also to make visitations to the sick and to the poor. The Bishop of Exeter was to be the official visitor. All members had to be communicants in the Church of England, and should a sister cease to be a member of the Anglican Communion, she automatically ceased to be a member of the community.

Lydia Sellon was aged twenty-eight when she established what was formally denominated "The Church of England Sisters of Mercy in Devonport". She was somewhat frail in health, but she was indomitable in spirit. She was not to assume that, as "Lady Superior", she was in any way exempt from the same tasks assumed by her colleagues. Because she was often willing to disregard some of the conventions of the day, certain elements in society regarded her behaviour as deviant. However, the poor and afflicted were soon to have other views, appreciating the efforts she made on their behalf.

The Lady Superior arranged the daily life of the sisters more or less as follows: rising early they received holy communion daily at eight, followed by meeting at nine, noon and then again in the afternoon for prayers, hymns and meditation. They generally attended evensong. Between the services they worked for about six hours. They had communal meals, silent times but also an hour or two a day for relaxation and socialising. In addition to the sisterhood, she created a group of pious individuals named the Company of the Love of Jesus who were divided into "watchers" or "choirs" who were committed to ensuring that there were constant prayers of intercession. On festive occasions holy communion was celebrated in the oratory of the orphanage. At Christmas time the pupils from the schools came with those from the orphanage to sing carols and join in the religious services at the residence of the community.

Despite assiduous parish visiting, the establishment of the orphanages for girls and the setting up of the College for Sailor Boys, the Sisters of Mercy did not receive universal acclaim. For one thing they were, perhaps, too closely associated with Pusey and the Tractarians. Traditional Protestants strongly disapproved of the latter and, in particular, what the conservatives felt was their Romanising tendencies. Hence, it is hardly surprising that Lydia Sellon became the object of antipathy in certain circles.

A local cleric named John Hatchard, in conjunction with the local press, decided that the Sisters of Mercy were a danger to the community. The critics managed to persuade three young women who had been residents in the home for girls to make statements concerning the religious practices they had witnessed. Hatchard decided to interview Lydia Sellon who, although not in the best of health, agreed to receive him. After the meeting Hatchard decided that the sisters were not papists *per se*, but that their conversion to Roman Catholicism was inevitable, and that they would take with them a number of their charges.

Hatchard sent a letter to the local newspaper in which he severely castigated Lydia Sellon for garbing her colleagues in "the habit", for using the term "sister" and above all arrogating to herself the title "Lady Superior". This letter was printed, conjoined with the statements of the three young women. Lydia Sellon herself wrote a rebuttal but the damage was done. Certain supporters of her work withdrew their patronage, among them Queen Adelaide. The Bishop of Exeter was not pleased to have such controversy in his diocese.

A fortnight after the press report, Bishop Phillpotts opened a formal enquiry. Hatchard, followed by the editor of the *Devonport Telegraph*, made statements, as did others. Initially Lydia Sellon was not present, but in the course of the hearing she made a dramatic entrance. The bishop allowed her to reply to her opponents, and in the course of her remarks demonstrated the triviality or the falsehood of her accusers. The hearing lasted some six hours and at its end the Bishop gave a ringing endorsement of the work of the Sisters and said of Lydia Sellon herself that she "might leave the room with the gratitude and approbation of all those whose good opinion she would value". Her local enemies were routed and the troop of Protestant bigots refuted. Generally speaking the London press was on her side. William Wordsworth, the aged poet laureate, dedicated a sonnet

To Miss Sellon –

The vestal princess of a Sisterhood
Who new no self and whom the selfish scorn,
She seeks a wilderness of weed and thorn,
And undiverted from her blessed mood
By keen reproach or blind ingratitude,
A wreath she twines of blossoms lowly born –
An amaranthine crown of flowers forlorn –
And hangs her garland on the Holy Road.

Sister of Mercy bravely thou hast won,
From men who winnow charity from faith,
The pharisaic sneer that treats as dross
The works ordained by faith. Pursue thy path,
Till at the last, thou hear the voice, "Well done,
Thou good and faithful servant of the Cross."

(Ambleside 22 February 1849)

Another poet, Robert Stephen Hawker, made famous by a description of his life as Vicar of Morwenstow, also wrote commending her in an ode entitled *A voice from the Place of St Morwenna in the Rocky Land*.

To recover from the strain of the inquiry, Lydia Sellon went to Oxford to stay with Pusey. She returned to Devonport when a terrible cholera epidemic broke out in the three towns of Devonport, Plymouth and Stoke. At once she offered herself and the sisters as nurses since the local medical authorities could not cope with the situation. She said to one local clergyman, "I am come to ask if you will accept the services of myself and my sisters in your parish . . . [she added] you must not look on us as mere ladies but as Sisters of Mercy – and the proper place for Sisters of Mercy is among the sick and the dying." The proferred help was accepted with alacrity.

With her usual efficiency she organised a proper nursing programme. She included her own colleagues, called upon some of the London sisters, and accepted the help of the local Roman Catholic nuns. A temporary hospital was erected, and the women lived and worked under harsh conditions for all of the summer and much of the autumn. Even Hatchard and the editor of the *Devonport Telegraph*, previously her critics, were lavish in their praise for her efforts. Uniformly the women were lauded, not only for their work as nurses but also as symbols of Christian charity. The London newspapers too were lavish in their praise, and money was collected to promote their efforts. A doctor observed, "There was a halo of sanctity around the persona of these calm sisters which inspired hope. . . ." Official thanks they did not receive despite all of the good work.

Lydia Sellon still had her critics. The editor of the *Devonport Telegraph*, who had praised her efforts, wrote an article in his newspaper implying that she had misappropriated funds sent to her for charitable purposes. To defend herself on this occasion she proceeded to sue the editor. Faced with legal proceedings, he apologised and agreed to pay the solicitors' fees. No sooner was this problem resolved than a clergyman accused the Sisters of Mercy of crypto-papism. Lydia Sellon did not bother to reply initially. However, when her opponents stated that the sisters were virtual slaves of the Lady Superior, and that they were bound to the order of an oath of secrecy, she did deign to make a response to his charges.

In the controversy over the decision in the Gorham case, the role played by Lord Campbell infuriated Lydia Sellon. He had participated in the legal proceedings and ruled against Bishop Phillpotts when the case finally reached the Judicial Committee of the Privy Council. She insisted that Campbell withdraw from the committee which actively supported the work of the Sisters of Mercy. He attempted to assuage her wrath but without success; she formally insisted on his expulsion. To protect his name, Lord Campbell gave copies of their correspondence to the press and the upshot was that the public was to see her not as an angel of mercy but as a harsh and vindictive individual.

Despite this imbroglio, the Sisters of Mercy continued to attract prospective members. Lydia Sellon was now to establish a sort of order of precedence for the postulants. Initially, and for a short period, the applicant was designated "visitor", once permitted to enter as a postulant, the term "novice" applied. After some period of time, she was called "child", finally and upon the vote of the choir sisters she could become a full member with the rank of "sister". There was no set time between the status of "child" and "sister", and it could be as long as a decade.

With more members of the community their activities could be extended. In 1851 there was a new school for girls, two houses established for destitute young females, and a soup kitchen set up to serve over one hundred meals a day. These were in addition to the five ragged schools, the orphanage and St George's College for Sailor Boys. There was also a home for old and disabled sailors.

Everything was planned and arranged by Lydia Sellon. Like Florence Nightingale later in the century, much was done from her sofa as she was crippled and forced to use a wheelchair. The evening classes for boys she continued to enjoy as much as she had done in earlier times. Although very much in charge, she had the nice ability to delegate, which made the work all proceed in a happy manner. It was not all work; the Sunday school while pious enough was not overly so, and the weekend except for the obligatory devotions was passed in reading, painting and intellectual conversations.

With enlargement came inevitable change. The original simple rules were more formalised and in 1851 she composed *The Seven Great Rules* but they were not put into effect for some five years. The sisterhood was now organised into three divisions: firstly, the Sisters of Mercy of the Holy Communion, which were in essence the original body of 1848; secondly, the Sisters of the Sacred Heart, who were an enclosed order and who occupied their time in prayer and contemplation; and thirdly, the Sisters of Charity of the Holy Ghost who were not part of the community directly but were very like the tertiaries of the Roman Catholic sisterhood. She even ordained a special garb, the first wore black, the second white and the third blue or grey.

She now felt the need to consider the erection of a building as a permanent centre for the sisters. With support from her family and various friends she acquired property, and employed the architect William Butterfield to design the building which in due course became known as St Dunstan's Abbeymere. The plans were ambitious as were most projects of Lydia Sellon. The focal centre was the abbey church but there was to be a library, a refectory, kitchens and dormitories. The cornerstone was laid by Bishop Phillpotts in October 1851. The event was marred by a group of rowdy Protestants who attacked invited guests, and the police had to be summoned.

Another crisis occurred when Augusta Wolfe, known to the community as Sister Winnifrede, abandoned her vocation and inspired a tract written by her brother-in-law, James Spurrell. Almost every aspect of the life was derided and attacked. The use of the canonical hours, candles and flowers in the oratory, the making of the sign of the cross, confession and penance were all described in a highly coloured manner. A reply had to be made, but Bishop Phillpotts, who now had some reservations about many of the activities, resigned as visitor. Lydia Sellon became acutely depressed, and briefly considered abandoning her life as a sister.

A series of tracts and negative comments followed. The first was by William Colles, who described her as "un-Protestant and un-English". Next Diana Campbell, a mentally unbalanced novice, described the Sisters of Mercy and its membership in a totally untruthful fashion. Before Lydia Sellon could make an adequate response Hobart Seymour, a well-known anti-Tractarian, delivered a lecture in which he attacked her theology describing her also as a despot, devious and a woman of dubious morality.

Friends came to her assistance. Spurrell's charges they refuted by proving that his informants were untruthful. Diana Campbell's veracity was questioned when it transpired that she had become a Roman Catholic, and had been directly involved in a felony. The press were to use these tracts for their own purposes; they titillated the taste of the public who vastly enjoyed reading of the iniquities of those who were trying to destroy the Established Church. Lydia Sellon attempted, and with some success, to retain an air of sanity in the midst of all of these difficulties.

It ought, however, to have been "Batten down the hatches" for no sooner were the attacks by Spurrell and Campbell beaten back than a new onslaught was launched. John Hatchard, despite having praised the sisters for their work during the cholera epidemic, returned to his stance of earlier days. On this occasion he asserted that the girls who lived in the orphanage under Lydia Sellon's supervision were required to attend confession. Among the principal objections the Protestants had against the Tractarians was the assumption that the latter believed in auricular confession. He said that George Prynne, the vicar of the parish church attended by the sisters, was the recipient of these confessions. Prynne was investigated by Bishop Phillpotts and totally exonerated. However, the former, an ally of Lydia Sellon, was caught up in the hostility directed against her.

A new opponent appeared on the scene. W. G. Cooksley, who was an Eton master, conjured up the facetious charge that Lydia Sellon maintained her authority by mesmerism. This was nonsense, but Cooksley insisted he was telling the truth and that the Jesuits liked the sisters because they were "such excellent nurseries for the Roman Catholic Church". Cooksley's pamphlet had wide circulation, going through five editions. Despite his challenging her to deny his remarks, she sensibly chose to say nothing. The year 1853 closed after twelve months of ceaseless battering with the opponents finally ending their attacks. For the next nine years a peace of sorts ensued.

The sisters moved into their new home at Abbeymere. The building was only semi-finished, but the edifice gave the community a sense of permanence. At this time Lydia Sellon took for herself the designation of abbess. She chose to recognise her earliest associates as eldress, the most senior of them was called Mother Eldress which she defined as prioress. Another colleague of long standing became Deane. These titles had mixed origins: from the Roman Catholic Church came abbess, from Anglicanism came deane – feminised dean, and from Dissent came eldress.

Late in the autumn Mother Lydia decided to send some of the community to the Crimea to assist Florence Nightingale. The experiment had mixed success owing to personality differences, but the sisters stayed twenty months. For their work little or no official recognition was made, but Florence Nightingale went on to become a national icon. At this time, too, arrangements were put in train for the London sisterhood – the Sisters of Holy Cross – to amalgamate with Devonport – the Sisters of Mercy. On her thirty-fifth birthday Lydia Sellon became the Lady Superior of the combined orders.

To celebrate the event later in the year a formal ceremony ensued. The sisters gave their vow of obedience to the Lady Superior. She, on this occasion, was garbed in a rather grand habit which owed its origin only remotely to abbatial clothing of Roman Catholic convents. New and more rigorous rules were promulgated at this time, in part to satisfy the sisters from the London community who were inclined to feel their Devonport associates overly casual. Dr Pusey approved of the amalgamation, and, on the occasion of the formal proceedings performed the religious rites demanded. A beneficent deity obviously supported all of these activities for the sisters now were the recipients of a generous benefaction, namely a large house in Bradford-on-Avon. Mother Lydia decided it would make an excellent residence for her Second Order. These sisters, while occupying themselves in the main with prayer and intercession, took up art printing and produced elegant volumes of Pusey's sermons and secular tomes of a serious nature.

The nine-year period of truce terminated in 1861. Margaret Goodman, who had been a probationer, left the community in high dudgeon when her dislike of the increasingly ritualistic nature of the sisterhood became apparent. In her rage she wrote a book entitled *Experience of an English Sister of Mercy*. This opus was a curious melange in that it was highly critical of Lydia Sellon accusing her of spiritual pride, selfishness, love of luxury but also recognising the nobility of her effort. Inevitably it was noted by the press with approval, but without the negative criticism expressed as had been the situation in earlier years. Margaret Goodman wrote a new version which was more violent in its criticism. Lydia Sellon once more decided "silence is golden" as a motto being aware that anything she might say could only seem to provide veracity to her critic's literary effusions.

St Dunstan's Abbey was virtually completed by 1863. It was to become Lydia Sellon's headquarters. With a pastoral staff and a special seat in the chapel there was no doubt who was the Lady Superior. Another conventual house was established at Ascot. This was named the Priory and endowed with funds from the Pusey family.

While reaping visible rewards for her efforts, her own health declined, and she had a paralytic stroke which very much lessened her mobility. She recovered in part but was never really totally cured. If somewhat physically infirm, her mental powers were in no way diminished. She planned to open a residence in Leeds for mill girls, but local sentiment was hostile to her work and nothing came of the project. She was minded to set up a priory in Norwich, but changed her mind and gave the property to the Sisters of Mount Calvary. In response to a request from the Bishop of Honolulu she agreed to organise a school and orphanage. Several sisters were sent as founding members. The story of this project was to be reported in full in a volume entitled *Five Years Church Work in the Kingdom of Hawaii*.

In the spring of 1866 Lydia Sellon, accompanied by Pusey and Brother Ignatius, who was anxious to reintroduce monasticism in England, embarked on an expedition to the Holy Land. En route the travellers learned of an outbreak of cholera in London, at once she and Pusey returned to England. They founded a hospital at Bethnal Green, and Lydia Sellon was once more to the fore organising the nursing. The cholera epidemic lasted some three months, and on this occasion she and the sisters were praised in a generous fashion.

Once again she became ill but refused to allow herself the luxury of a modified existence. Moreover, she responded to an invitation of Queen Emma of Hawaii by deciding to visit the islands herself. On 15 February 1867 she and six companions left England. They sailed to Panama, crossed the isthmus by train, and sailed north to San Francisco where they embarked anew for the trans-Pacific voyage. The journey from England took ten weeks, and when they landed at the end of March they were greeted by a deputation of local grandees and clergy. They were housed in a former residence of Queen Emma and lavishly entertained. Plans for a new school had been sent in advance and on Ascension Day there was a special celebration. Queen Emma who had been made an associate of the Society of the Holy

Trinity was present, as were members of her family. A week after the formal dedication of St Andrew's Priory, Lydia Sellon, three of her companions and three local girls departed for England. The school and the convent generally prospered, initially however the American residents were somewhat hostile, seeing the two institutions as a stalking horse for British imperial pretensions to annex the Sandwich Islands.

Once back at Ascot where she and Mother Eldress Catherine were in residence, they found a relative degree of calm. Militant Protestant activity was generally directed to the various cases concerning ritual that were to find their way to the Privy Council. Lydia Sellon was never a ritualist *per se*, and while the sisters took holy communion every day, and kept the so-called Benedictine rules of hours, the services were strictly in accord with the Book of Common Prayer of 1662.

In the autumn of 1876 a real personal crisis ensued. For some unknown reason Mother Eldress Catherine, one of the most senior of her sisters and very probably Lydia Sellon's best friend, left the community. She was later to become a Roman Catholic and to die as one of the Sisters of the Institute of the Virgin Mary. The defection of this dear companion was a truly devastating blow. Lydia Sellon was already very ill. She made her will on 2 October 1876, prior to her demise named Sister Bertha Turnbull as her successor. She died on 20 November 1876 aged fifty-four after being associated with the Devonport community for some twenty-eight years. Edward Pusey was with her on her deathbed, he had been her priest, her confidante, her friend and constant support in life.

Her funeral was as she had wished. The body was conveyed to Ascot Priory, there was a vigil of the dead and a requiem mass. She was buried in the cemetery of the Ascot Priory. Her headstone was a simple one, a stone cross. The secular press was generous in its commendation. *The Times* for example gave her special credit not only for her role in the Devonport community but also for her efforts to ensure the establishment of other sisterhoods. Later she was to be the recipient of a personal tribute in the Lower House of Convocation. At long last the establishment accepted her.

Regretfully she left the order with many problems not only personal but also financial which took some five years to resolve. She and Mother Eldress Catherine had administered in a highly personal fashion, and they had not allowed the financial side to deter them from any course of action they deemed necessary. Pusey and Mother Bertha finally managed to get the Society of the Most Holy Trinity on a proper footing.

Lydia Sellon has provoked considerable argument as to her contribution and significance to religious life. There are some who consider her as a saint, that she lived a life of selfless service who experienced undue calumny and persecution. Owen Chadwick regards her as one of the "indomitables of Victorian womanhood". To others she appears to be domineering, self-righteous, autocratic, authoritarian and selfish. She has been seen by some as a proto-feminist and an early advocate of Anglican social conscience. At the same time she was very much of her time and background being class conscious; few if any working class women were admitted to full sisterhood. She was somewhat of a romantic, and looked back to earlier times in her interpretation of conventual life. It must be recognised that she was fearless in adversity and also in facing the possible personal risks such as what could ensue during the cholera in Devonport. She was disciplined herself and expected obedience from her inferiors. She did not share power; the order was once described as "a despotic monarchy without a parliament". Her opponents regarded her as a "Romaniser" yet in fact she remained a traditional Anglican in her personal worship.

It must be recognised that not the least of her success was to assume rights and powers which Victorian society had allocated only to men and hence she was a rebel. She had a mission, but she could not have accomplished what she did if she had been too gentle, too self-effacing. Good deeds require rather more than simple goodness. She used strong measures when necessary but all crusaders must act in such a way. Lydia Sellon made the Anglican sisterhoods a reality. For a century and a half her work has survived. Her mission did not fail because of what she did to Anglicanism; rather the sense of vocation changed in the twentieth century. Women could make their way in the world, the alleviation of poverty, ignorance and social deprivation became a secular matter. The church and society abandoned Lydia Sellon, she did not abandon them. "One feels that she must have been a very lonely soul, born out of due time, fighting battles with few at her side upon whom she could rely in times of crisis."

Mary Baker Eddy

New England in the first quarter of the nineteenth century was little different from what it had been at the time of the revolution. Life was relatively simple; "the dark satanic mills" had not yet marred the charms of the rural landscape, as they were to do as the century progressed. Traditional Calvinist belief still probably dominated much of the thinking although challenged by Unitarianism and Transcendentalism.

The village of Bow in New Hampshire could readily serve as the model community for later writers seeking to evoke, in a more worldly age, the charms of the simple life. The orthodoxy of religious thought determined the moral character of the community, but the relative rigidity of belief was leavened by the ideas of progress and democracy. The Yankee denizens with such concepts could readily regard themselves as the *beau idéal* citizens of the republic.

Mary Morse Baker was born in 1821. She was the sixth and youngest child of Noah and Abigail Baker. ("Eddy", which is the name most commonly associated with her she assumed upon marriage to her third husband.) As a child Mary Baker was somewhat frail, but her ailments were never precisely defined. Her general malaise was such that she was indulged by her parents and brothers and sisters. Her attendance at school was irregular, but her second brother, Albert, took it upon himself to encourage her general reading. He introduced her to such compilations as *The English Reader*, which ensured that she became acquainted with the accepted best prose and poetry of the day.

Like many of her contemporaries in the 1830s and 1840s, she amused herself in writing poetry or what passed for poetry. These literary effusions, of no great merit, were decidedly typical of the period. One brief example will serve to illustrate this fact.

> Love, Lady Love
> There is a joy in loving
> But sigh not when you find
> That man is fond of roving
> He like the summer bee

Takes wings through beauty's bowers
And knows not where to choose
Among so many flowers
Love, Lady Love

Laetitia Elizabeth Landon or Marguerite Blessington would have appreciated such sentiments and written in a not dissimilar fashion.

Although she was accepted as a full member of the Sanbornton Congregational Church – the family had acquired a new home in Sanbornton when she was fifteen – she was somewhat unorthodox in her personal beliefs. She declined to accept the generally assumed Calvinism, and found it impossible to believe that salvation was the privilege of the few. It was not the stern judgemental Jehovah but rather the loving Father that appealed to her.

When she was twenty-two she married George Glover. The latter, although born in New Hampshire, had business interests in South Carolina. Glover, according to report, was friendly and gregarious with a positive and optimistic outlook on life. Mary Baker knew that her new life would be very different from that previously experienced.

Following their marriage the young couple made their home in Wilmington, North Carolina. The bride's health improved, and good prospects for the future seemed to be assured. Sadly, such was not to be the case. Glover's business interests fell into difficulties, but far worse the young man caught yellow fever and expired. He died in June 1844 after only six months of marriage. His widow was left virtually penniless, and, moreover, she was pregnant. The obvious solution was for her to return to New Hampshire where she could expect to be supported by her family.

Mary Glover's child was born on 12 September 1844. He was christened George Washington Glover after his late father. The infant was put into the care of Mabola Sanborn since his mother was too frail to care for him properly. The subsequent story of George Washington Glover is a somewhat melancholy one. Mary Glover was not really a maternal person. The boy was farmed out for much of the next decade. When he was aged eleven it was decided that he should accompany his foster parents when they moved to one of the western states.

Although in later years Mary Baker Eddy seems to have convinced herself that she had been duped by others into agreeing to this arrangement, this was not true. In fact, this was a most satisfactory situation for her. Mother and son were not to meet for some two decades.

Mary Glover's own life took a turn for the better when she met Daniel Patterson. He was handsome, gregarious and appeared reasonably prosperous. He was a dentist with a decent practice, and marriage to him would ensure a happy and secure future. His financial situation was, however, not what it seemed, and under a façade of respectability the newly married couple were very impoverished. Since she was unable to participate as an equal in the local society, she became something of a recluse. To occupy her time she entertained herself reading the Bible and she, like the mediaeval contemplatives, fixed her mind on other-worldly matters to escape from the miseries of her present situation.

Whatever the exigencies of her existence she experienced at this time, she seems to have retained a generally orthodox theology. She had no doubts about the eternal life in the hereafter being convinced that she would rejoin her deceased mother and favourite brother. She was not attracted to spiritualism, but she was uncritical about the Fox sisters. At no time was she tempted to attempt contact with "the other side", and later, in fact, she was to reject spiritualism totally.

In September 1859, the fortunes of the Pattersons reached their nadir, their furniture went to auction and their property was sold. They were reduced to the indignity of boarding house life. In an attempt to alleviate the situation, Mary Patterson made modest contributions to various newspapers. Her endeavours had some success and she received a little money for her efforts.

The outbreak of the Civil War brought her in contact with her son. She had heard nothing from him for a decade. He wrote that he had joined an infantry regiment in Wisconsin. She seems to have been relatively pleased to have news of him, but was not overly encouraging and did little more than to acknowledge receipt of his letter.

She continued to be a semi-invalid and, in an attempt to find a cure, took an interest in homeopathic medicine of various sorts. One form of treatment that she tried was to place herself in the care of a hydropathic practitioner. His efforts on her behalf were not particularly successful. While experiencing the hydropathic treatment, she learned about the work of Phineas Quimby who, according to what she read, seemed to have almost miraculous powers.

What was Quimby's method exactly? He asserted that patients were not cured by drugs or any medicines but through something quite different. He noted that "Disease is the name of the disturbance of the fluids in the mind." Initially he had believed that cures could be effected through mesmerism, and that his patients would need to be hypnotised, but ultimately he rejected this idea. Rather he used suggestion and a sort of physical manipulation which embodied what he called "animal magnetism". Apparently a force passed from Quimby to the patient, and that in consequence he could explain the nature of the illness. By so doing he could effect a cure by ensuring the patient knew "the truth" of the particular malaise. A later writer noted that Quimby seems to have cured disease through the mind. To be effective the patient had to have implicit faith, and to believe there was no pain. Quimby was to play a special role in the ultimate teachings of Mary Baker Eddy.

It appeared as if Quimby were able to bring about an improvement in Mary Patterson's health after she had visited him in Portland, Maine. She had no doubts of the effectiveness of his "method". She collected Quimby's ephemeral writings, and enthusiastically wrote and even delivered some lectures to popularise his activities. She even attempted to use his so-called "transference" practice herself on some friends and acquaintances with considerable success. She did not feel totally secure in these activities, and was in constant contact with Quimby to ensure that somehow she herself did not fall into ill health. This relationship came to an end when he died in January 1866 and she felt very bereft indeed.

However, a month later an event occurred which was to change her life. She had a serious accident, and fears were expressed that she would die. She did not die, but apparently experienced something very unusual for it was from this time forward one can date her special mission. She now believed that fear, pain and death were irrelevant and that "this life being the sole reality of existence" and that everything in it being "spiritual, divine, immortal and wholly good".

Her domestic life did not reflect her renewed vigour. Patterson was notoriously unfaithful, and she finally informed him they would have to part. He agreed to the separation possibly in the belief that it was only temporary but he was wrong, and they were divorced seven years later. He lived until 1896 and made nothing of his life. His wife's decision was perhaps somewhat unforgiving, but she gained a freedom without which she could never have undertaken the great mission for which she became so famous.

With no husband and no further contact with her son, Mary Patterson was able to occupy herself as she chose. She began to put her thoughts into an organised form. She rejected Quimby's idea that the human mind healed and replaced it with the concept that God was the healer; that it was a divine principle not a human one. Man, she said, was made in God's image, a spiritual idea that is perfect and that in his likeness of God "wholly good and wholly spirit".

Her first convert was Hiram Cofts. He and his wife were impressed by her seeming healing powers, and he asked to become her pupil. Initially she was reluctant to accept him, but in due course she did so. He became a professional healer. The agreeable relationship between teacher and student did not long continue. The two parted in an acrimonious fashion.

After moving to Amesbury Mary Glover, as she now called herself, was to acquire two new disciples. One, Sarah Bingley, was to practice as a healer using her teacher's method for some three decades. The other was Richard Kennedy. He was to be the first of a series of youthful male protégés, almost all of whom were to have disagreements with their mentor. Richard Kennedy became an accomplished healer, and his success brought her to the attention of other potential pupils. Inevitably, not all were satisfied with her tuition. For example, Wallace Wright, initially a success, had doubts of the efficacy of her instruction and when reproved by her he became angry. The upshot was that he wrote a letter to *The Lynn Transcript* declaring that her so-called "moral science" was but a form of mesmerism. The matter might have ended there – she totally rejected his remarks – but Richard Kennedy himself agreed with Wright and therefore all contact between Mary Glover and her erstwhile protégé ended. Such schisms were to become part and parcel of the whole development of Christian Science. Mary Glover was to require a total commitment to her teachings, any deviation meant disloyalty and ultimately expulsion.

The one positive result of the quarrel was that she was able to cast aside permanently any influence Quimby might have had on her formerly, magnetism and mesmerism were to be replaced by her own very personal religious beliefs. It was obvious that some sort of corpus evolve for the future. She began to write what was to be her major opus under the title *Science and Health*. It was published in October 1875. By then she had bought a house in Lynn, Massachusetts, had some real adherents and had received a form of approbation from Bronson Alcott. The reviewers in general seem to have greeted her book in a favourable fashion. She could congratulate herself on her modest successes.

What was she like? She was in her early fifties having retained her good looks and her girlish figure. She was noticeable for her attractive appearance and general stylishness. Not for her were the drab colours generally associated with middle-aged females; rather she selected blues, mauves, pinks and shades of green. Her dresses were not plain and severe but embellished with bows and flounces with touches of lace at the neck and wrists. Her hair was not yet grey but a light brown in colour and always handsomely coiffed. Middle-aged women, particularly if they have good looks and intelligence, are very attractive to younger men. Mary Glover was to be no exception.

At this juncture, three relatively youthful admirers entered her life. The first was Daniel Spofford who ultimately became a most successful healer. He was to fall in love with her, and would have liked to marry her if he had been able to divorce his wife, which he could not do. The second was George Barry who unlike Spofford was content to exist in the role of "son". He appears to have been useful acting as an amanuensis, and coping with domestic affairs. He always addressed Mary Glover as "Mother". The third individual was Asa Gilbert Eddy, and he was to have a role much more important than the other two.

In March 1876 Asa Gilbert Eddy enrolled in one of her classes. He quickly became totally committed to a belief in Christian Science. Indeed, on a later occasion, Mary Glover was to say that he was the first person other than herself to designate himself as such. He was apparently a thoroughly nice person with an endearing character. He could under no circumstances be thought scintillating, but he was sociable and kind. He proposed to her and she accepted, and they were married on 1 January 1877 in a quiet and unostentatious fashion.

The reaction of the other two swains was mixed. Barry was quietly accepting while Spofford was deeply wounded. While Barry's position in the domestic life of the household was necessarily lessened, Spofford continued, despite his jealousy, to be in favour, and he was charged with the responsibility of the publication and sales of *Science and Health*. Financial difficulties ensued and the anticipated new edition did not appear. On 20 December 1877 he was formally expelled from the Christian Science Association. He was given a month to submit to direction and to admit error, but he declined to do so. A second vote was taken which re-affirmed the first, he was officially expelled for what was called "immorality". This word in the vocabulary of Mary Baker Eddy meant "immorality of belief". Attempts were made by friends of both parties to patch up the quarrel, but without success.

In the summer of 1879 Mary Baker Eddy formally established the Church of Christ Scientist. The basic tenets of the church can be summarised under the general title "Scientific Statements of Being". Firstly, "There is no life, truth, intelligence nor substance in matter."

Secondly, "All is infinite mind and its infinite manifestation, for God is all in all." Thirdly, "Spirit is immortal truth; matter is mortal error." Fourthly, "Spirit is the real and eternal; matter is the unreal and temporal." Fifthly, "Spirit is God, and man is His image and likeness." Lastly, "Therefore man is not material; he is spiritual." She was to write, "erring finite human mind has an absolute need of something beyond itself for its redemption and healing." This "healing" is from sin primarily and disease secondary; healing is not just a bodily change but an aspect of full salvation from the flesh as well. She rejected the idea that healing was an end in itself, healing was one essential aspect of salvation.

Certain words, which she used in her correspondence and writings, served to express ideas in a sort of shorthand form. The first was "chemicalise", which meant an individual's behaviour was irritating, obdurate and tactless, and it required admonishment. The second was "immorality", which implied opposition to the ideas and leadership of Mary Baker Eddy. Individuals who were deviationists were expelled from the society under the term "immorality". The third word was "malpractice". This was a sort of mesmeric or animal magnetism expressed and directed to another to cause acute distress. Mary Baker Eddy was to aver that "malpractice" was the cause of her husband's death.

In June 1882 her husband Gilbert Eddy died. It was a devastating blow; she was convinced that he was the victim of mesmerism and malicious malpractice all emanating from the machinations of those who opposed her leadership. A medical practitioner, Rufus King Noyes, one who was not opposed to the idea of metaphysical healing, was convinced rather that Gilbert Eddy had succumbed to a fatal heart attack. She rejected Noyes's opinion completely. She believed that mesmeric poison had murdered her husband.

After a brief sojourn away from Boston, she returned, determined to continue her teachings. She had asked her son to come and stay – they had met again a few years previously though the encounter was only marginally successful – but he declined to accept her invitation. The orthodox religious bodies initially had paid scant attention to her teachings, but with success, criticism and attacks became more common. One critic's comment annoyed her particularly in that he associated her with Madame Blavatsky. As a result, she gave a public lecture in Boston in which she firmly rejected such an idea. To promote and protect her teachings, she would have to define her ideas specifically. She would recruit persons who could carry the message.

The potential teachers were carefully selected by Mary Baker Eddy herself, and were to be the recipients of the message in twelve lessons. The neophytes were to study the writings of the leader and to heal since they had experienced truth and could set others free. Mary Baker Eddy inspired her pupils, as a mentor she praised and admonished. Of course, there were those who failed, who fell into "malicious mesmerism" or "malpractice" and per force became separated from her society. Her *Journal of Christian Science* became the principal source for the dissemination of her ideas and precepts. Her close assistant and editor was James Harvey Wiggin who never himself became a Christian Scientist, but he was able to revise her writings in a professional fashion, thereby to ensure that her ideas were expressed in a more cogent manner.

Although George Washington Glover had rejected his mother's request to come to Boston when his stepfather Gilbert Eddy died, he and his wife and children came for a lengthy sojourn in 1887. Like the earlier visit, this present one was not overly happy, and he and his family were easily persuaded after some six months to return to South Dakota. His mother provided the funds for the journey; indeed, over the years she continued to augment the resources of her son, which enabled him to live comfortably. However, after this visit contacts between Mary Baker Eddy and George Washington Glover continued but in a restrained fashion.

In 1889, she closed the Massachusetts College of Metaphysical Science, which she had established a few years previously. She also officially dissolved the Christian Science Association, and declared that she had ceased all pastoral duties. She announced that she was retiring from Boston. Had her critics triumphed and driven her into exile? The crucial clue to the future had they but known where to look was the fact that she had acquired land in that part of Boston known as "Back Bay" where in the fullness of time she was to build the great edifice, "The Mother Church".

She moved to Concord in New Hampshire establishing herself in a pleasant rural situation. She was now 68 years of age, still attractive and stylish in dress. Her special air of serenity made her most agreeable company. She proceeded to produce a new and revised text of *Science and Health*. This was to become the authoritative version. Her life was comfortable, friends ensured that she had an adequate income and the household consisted of Calvin Frye, her secretary, a cook, a housekeeper and a gardener. In addition, from time to time her adopted son Ebenezer – she called him "Benny"-Foster Eddy – lived with her.

Deviating Voices

This young man had followed another protégé, William Gill, in her affections. Gill was essentially a person of little real understanding and after the most inevitable quarrel was expelled from the Society for the usual reasons. Benny Eddy regarded Mary Baker Eddy – "Mother" as he called her – with obvious affection. Initially the relationship was a happy one, but almost inevitably there was to be friction between the two of them. He began to act as if he were the anointed successor, and implied that "Mother" was a fragile being, mildly senile who required his directing hand. In fact, she allowed him little real power, real authority other than her own was vested in the three associates or trustees in Boston.

At the Columbian Exhibition in Chicago in 1893, there was a world congress of Christian Scientists. Some four thousand people attended. She did not personally address the assembly preferring to have a chosen friend, Judge Septimus Hannon, deliver the speech which she had written. The Christian Science congress was part of a larger body, the Parliament of Religions, which was convened at the same time. The significance of this joint assembly assured that Christian Science could be seen as part of a global movement; it was no longer an isolated and obscure sect.

The decision to erect what was "The Mother Church" was taken early the next year. Forty friends – students, teachers and believers – each contributed one thousand dollars to defray expenses. The building was completed by late December of that year and the first service was held on the thirtieth of the month. She, herself, was not present, and on the formal dedication she was again absent. The speech which she had written for this occasion was read on her behalf by Henrietta Clark, a professional elocutionist. Her adopted son was much displeased by this procedure as he had hoped to be the centre of attention himself. By excluding him in this fashion "Mother" knew precisely what she was doing and why.

Her initial visit occurred in April and it was a moment of triumph. The huge building was the visible proof of her success. On this occasion she conducted a form of service incorporating a favourite hymn and the ninety-first psalm. To add to the sense of occasion she actually arranged to sleep in one of the side rooms in the church. Two months later on a second visit she delivered a short homily. The topic of the discourse was not one of self-congratulation, but rather on repentance and sin. There never seems to have been much humour or lightness in her public commentary. Perhaps the only occasion was when she decided to have the Westminster chimes shut off at night as she observed the purpose of Christian Science was not to give the neighbours sleepless nights.

In the midst of these triumphs the relationship between Foster Eddy – "Benny" – and herself was to end. Initially she tried to keep something of the earliest affection for him, but finally recognised that he did not have the necessary capacity to sustain any real position in the church or in her life. She banished him from Concord and observed, "Flattery and pleasure seeking." He ceased to be regarded as a son, and only emerged from the shadows a few years later and in a somewhat despicable fashion. Each protégé, and they were inevitably younger men, brought to her a sense of renewal, each must owe everything to her and if the individual attempted any form of independence for whatever reason, he was cast into outer darkness. The fall of Lucifer could not have been more complete.

Christian Science was no longer just a North American phenomenon. In 1897, a church was formally inaugurated in England and soon after in Australia and New Zealand. Branches were to be found also in France and Germany. In the latter, a somewhat nationalistic organisation was to develop which was not entirely in keeping with the announced precepts of "The Mother Church". There were few inroads made in the Latin countries as the Roman Catholic hierarchy regarded Christian Science as a most dangerous heresy.

Success brought more critics inevitably. One of her most famous opponents was Mark Twain. His hostility arose in no small part because he had hoped that through Christian Science he might find a cure for his daughter's infirmities. Sadly this did not occur. In his anger, he felt that Mary Baker Eddy had traded on hope for her own nefarious purposes. He decided she was a charlatan who had acquired wealth and power through devious means. He felt it was hypocritical that she allowed herself to be addressed as "Mother" thereby usurping the Virgin Mary herself. He regarded her as being intellectually pretentious, her writings superficial and he observed, "She has no more intellect than a tadpole, until she comes to business she is a marvel."

The turn of the century saw the First Church of Christ Scientist in a situation of almost euphoric prosperity. The Church did not however participate in social, cultural or philanthropic activities, the membership were to be active in such matters as individuals not as the Church itself. She herself was relatively generous with donations to selected charities; she lent her name to promote international well being such as The Hague Peace Conference, but always as herself alone. She did, however, allow the French government to name her as an *officier d'Académie*.

Public admiration brought her to the attention of the gutter press. Articles that appeared in *The New York World* implied that she was either senile or worse, that the person who purported to be "the Concord Saint" was an impostor. She actually allowed herself to be interviewed, but when the reporters were received, they were very chagrined to find her very much in charge of herself and the church. *McClures Journal*, a well-known muck-raking periodical, also published some very negative commentary. These articles were written by the author Willa Cather and ultimately appeared in a book. The church in due course acquired the manuscript and arranged also that a number of copies of *The Life of Mary Baker Eddy and the History of Christian Science* were deliberately destroyed.

A further attack on Mary Baker Eddy was conjured up by William Chandler, who declared she was incompetent to handle her own affairs. He enlisted the support of George Washington Glover. Ebenezer Foster Eddy also joined this camarilla. A judicial suit ensued. The court-appointed witnesses reported that she was totally sane and totally able to manage her own affairs. Chandler, Glover and Eddy gained nothing, and were regarded by the public at large as villainous schemers preying on an old woman. They also had to pay all of the court costs.

Mary Baker Eddy surprisingly forgave George Glover and Ebenezer Foster Eddy. To the former she gave nearly a quarter of a million dollars and to the latter some fifty thousand. Both had to agree that neither would contest her will. Sensibly, they accepted her proposition. George Washington Glover returned to South Dakota, Foster Eddy retired to rural Vermont. Neither played any further role in her life and both were extremely lucky to receive anything from her, considering their behaviour.

After the conclusion of the case, she abandoned her home in Concord and bought a mansion in Boston. At the same time she decided to become the publisher of a newspaper that was to cover international affairs and intellectual and cultural matters. *The Christian Science Monitor*, as the newspaper was called, was to become one of the most respected in the United States. The editorial board over the years were to maintain the highest standards, and the paper was recognised as being intellectually stimulating.

Her final year was one of unusual calm. She had rejected all efforts from her followers to write her memoirs, saying, "As Mary Baker

Eddy I am the weakest of mortals, but as the Discoverer and Founder of Christian Science I am the bone and sinew of the world." She retained to the last her stylish outward appearance. Death *per se* meant nothing to her, she was totally serene. She died on 3 December 1910 and was buried in Mount Auburn Cemetery in Cambridge, Massachusetts. Her detractors asserted that in her tomb was a telephone so that she could communicate with the world on some occasion upon her return.

Mary Baker Eddy was a curious individual. She had what might be described as a sort of "divine madness". That she was paranoid cannot be denied; that she was despotic and autocratic can be seen in her treatment of her church and her protégés. Disobedience to the orders of the leader was followed by instant punishment, the ultimate being banishment from her presence. Her role as "Mother" allowed her to express herself in the pretence of moral and intellectual justification. She was able to disguise personal hostility in the guise of mentor. She frequently was purely whimsical in her metaphysical pronouncements and the logicality of her commentary quite lacking. She used the language of the philosopher or the scientist but tended to put her own gloss on whatever she wrote. *Science and Health* contained all that one needed to know; through its author's writings one became aware of the truth.

At the time of her demise there were some 50,000 members of the Church, a quarter of a century earlier there had been about 60. The Church came to be regarded as a comfortable billet of the middle classes but how does one account for Lady Astor, the actress Joyce Grenfell, Lord Lothian, sometime British ambassador to the United States, and Sir James Butler, an eminent Cambridge historian?

Christian Science has a minor role in feminist history. Activity in the church is one in which women have taken a major role. Mary Baker Eddy was often commended in her own day for her brilliant organisational skills which were generally assumed to be masculine attributes. Her successes were not due to "sweetness and light". Revolutionaries, and she was a revolutionary, do not object to destroy the deviant in the name of the cause. The latter is more important than any individual, except perhaps for the leader, and she was always the leader.

Helena Petrovna Blavatsky

Russia in the first half of the nineteenth century was regarded by the majority of European society as being a world apart. The country, despite the efforts of Peter the Great and his brilliant successor Catherine the Second, was somehow different, and seemed to many travellers only semi-civilised. The vast distances, the vagaries of climate and the polyglot population all tended to emphasise that the Russian Empire was only peripherally, at best, part of the civilised world. Socially there were essentially only two classes of society, the aristocrat and the peasant – an urban middle class of sorts existed in a few towns and cities but it was really unimportant. Over all of this country was the autocrat embodied for a quarter of a century by the Tsar Nicholas the First.

Helena Petrovna von Hahn – better remembered as Madame Blavatsky – was born on 12 August 1831. Her father, Peter Alexyevitch von Hahn, was an army officer. The von Hahns had originally been part of the Baltic gentry, sometimes referred to as the "Baltic Germans". Originating in Mecklenbourg the von Hahns had entered the Russian service in the eighteenth century. Her mother, Helena Andreyevna Fadeyev, was the daughter of a senior civil servant. She was only sixteen years when she married in 1830; her husband was some fourteen years older. Legend has it that it was a love match and that it had all of the romantic elements in the poetry of Pushkin.

Shortly after the wedding the bride and groom were to be separated. He was ordered to rejoin his regiment, which was sent to repress the Polish uprising of 1830. The young bride returned to live with her parents at Ekaterinoslav, and it was here that Helena Petrovna was born. The infant was deemed to have little chance of survival for the cholera was endemic, but she confounded all prognostications to the contrary. At her christening, her three-year-old aunt accidentally set fire to the officiating priest's robes – all of the participants except the infant were holding candles – with the result that he was very severely burned. The superstitious peasantry regarded the event as an evil omen, and prognosticated that the child would have a life full of difficulty.

With the restoration of Russian authority in Poland, Peter von Hahn and his family were re-united. They were to move from one garrison town to another. Two other children were to be born in quick succession, but only the daughter survived. The elder of the von Hahn children apparently was not particularly docile or agreeable. She had frequent temper tantrums and violent unpredictable rages. The story is told that she frightened a young serf who had annoyed her when she screamed at him that a *roussalka* was after him. He fled and apparently fell into a stream and was drowned. Officially, it was deemed to have been an accident, but the peasants were convinced that the little girl had caused his demise by occult powers.

Life in the limited society of the garrison town came to an end in 1837 when the von Hahns moved to St Petersburg. Helena Petrovna von Hahn found the society of the imperial capital much to her liking. Her life was not just one round of dinners, receptions and balls for she discovered that she had a talent for writing popular fiction. She was very successful, and her reputation among the literati was not inconsiderable. In all she was to be the author of eleven major novels and several novellas. She seems to have espoused women's rights in a modest manner and also to have promoted women's education. Like Charlotte Bronte and her sisters, she used a pseudonym, "Zenaida R-Va".

After several years serving in the garrison in St Petersburg, Peter von Hahn was sent to the Ukraine. His wife and daughters did not accompany him, preferring to join her parents. Helena Andreyevna's health declined, she probably had tuberculosis, and she died aged 28 on 6 July 1842. Her last words were supposedly directed to her elder daughter, "Ah well perhaps it is best that I am dying so at least I shall be spared what befalls Helena. Of one thing I am certain her life will not be as that of other women and she will have much to suffer." It is said that the dying have the gift of prophecy, and certainly Helena Petrovna's mother final words were very prescient indeed.

The Fadeyevs undertook to care for the von Hahn children. There were now three, two girls and a boy, the latter born in 1840. Two of the preceptresses, Anna Kulavein and Augusta Jeffries, were successful in ensuring that the young von Hahns were reasonably educated as befitted their social class. Helena Petrovna was not a bookish child but she had a certain talent for languages and was to be fluent in French, German and English as well as her native Russian.

Some time later in 1844 or early 1845 Peter von Hahn decided to make a trip to England and he arranged for his elder daughter to accompany him. The travellers stayed in London and made several excursions. It was at this time she avowed that her father began to appreciate her musical talents, and found several good teachers for her in London She later claimed to have had lessons from the distinguished composer and conductor Ignaz Moscheles, and asserted on a later occasion that she had played duets with Clara Schumann though there is no reliable evidence for the truth of these statements.

Upon their return they went to Saratov but shortly thereafter her grandparents, the Fadeyevs, were to move to Tiflis. Initially the von Hahns were to reside with their aunt Catherine Witte. Von Hahn returned to his military duties. After a short period of time Catherine Witte, her husband Yuli and her son Sergius – he was later to be Prime Minister in the reign of Emperor Nicholas II – and the von Hahn children moved to Tiflis. Andrei Fadeyev lived in considerable style in the Georgian capital in the palace belonging to the Chavchavadzes, one of the country's most historic families. The Kingdom of Georgia had only been part of the Russian Empire for about half a century and its capital Tiflis was an odd amalgam of Russian and semi-Asiatic society. The local people had their own language and their own autonomous branch of the Orthodox Church.

At sixteen Helena Petrovna von Hahn was a somewhat truculent young woman. She was decidedly plain with a Kalmuch (semi-Asiatic) face, a dumpy figure, and rather frizzy hair but her eyes were arresting. She declined to participate in the polite circles of her grandparents, observing, "I hate dress and civilised society, I despise a ballroom." Although not of a literary turn of mind, she seems to have enjoyed reading curious books concerned with mediaeval folk tales, the writings of mystics, alchemists and cabbalists. All of this literature she felt reinforced her special sense of occult powers. She attracted the attention of Prince Alexander Galitzine who like her was interested in the occult, but her family did not encourage him as a suitor. His family were thought to be excessively mystical and somewhat eccentric and Prince Alexander apparently inherited these undesirable characteristics. Helena Petrovna in later years said they were engaged, but the machinations of Andrei Fadeyev prevent the marriage and Prince Alexander was forced to leave Tiflis.

Among those who also found her interesting and attractive in an exotic sort of fashion was Nikifor Vassilievich Blavatsky, the deputy governor of Erevan in Armenia. He was a friend of the Fadeyev family and like them part of the state service. He was over twenty years her senior, and she derisively referred to him as "old man".

Initially, she totally rebuffed his attentions but apparently she seems to have changed her mind when her governess taunted her with the comment that she was so plain and so ill-natured that she could never find a spouse just like "the plumeless raven". Facing such a challenge, Helena Petrovna made a complete *volte face* and accepted Blavatsky's proposal. The Fadeyev family were delighted by her decision, but she had second thoughts and tried in vain to break off the engagement. From all reports, Nikifor Blavatsky was just a very decent man who was prepared to tolerate the vagaries of the individual with whom he had fallen in love.

The wedding took place in June 1849 with her grandparents, brother and sister and various other relations in attendance. Evidently, the family wished to ensure that Helena Petrovna would go through with the ceremony; hence the large family gathering. According to Madame Yermolova, a family friend, Helena Petrovna had actually tried to run away to join Prince Galitzine but much to her chagrin he apparently had lost all interest in her.

The marriage was to be a complete failure. It may well be that it was never consummated, and within a short space of time the young bride hated her middle-aged husband. After only a few months she decamped and returned to Tiflis. Nikifor Blavatsky, always the perfect gentleman, never talked about his wife and her aberrant behaviour; however, some years later he attempted to have his marriage annulled, but for reasons unknown does not seem to have been successful.

The Fadeyev family were horrified at Helena Petrovna's decision to leave her husband, and she was received without any sort of enthusiasm. After discussions with the grandparents, she agreed to join her father who was living in St Petersburg. It is unclear whether her relations thought that somehow the marriage could be annulled or that a divorce could be obtained through von Hahn's influence in the imperial capital.

The tales that she was to tell of her life of the next quarter century are confusing and certainly incapable of being proved. Her own veracity, even at the best of times, was never overly reliable. It seems, and everyone is in general agreement, that she evaded her travel companions appointed by her grandfather and made her way to Constantinople. Her cousin Sergius Witte says in his memoirs that she became a circus rider. As she had no visible sign of support, this may even be possible.

She herself was to say that in due course she left Constantinople and went on to Cairo. Again, without evidence to the contrary this may be true. While in Cairo she struck up an acquaintance with an American artist named Alfred Lawson Rowson. He and she were to become intimate friends; he may well have actually proposed to her but she declined to marry him. Indeed, she could not do so without committing bigamy as she was still married to Blavatsky. She liked Rowson as a companion, but did not wish him to be a husband or, indeed, a lover. She accepted a position as companion to a Countess Kissilev with whom she remained for a few months. Later she appears to have had a similar situation in the household of a Princess Bagration.

She and the Princess travelled extensively and in 1851 they went to London. While there like most visitors they went to The Great Exhibition. The principal event of her stay was, as she noted, that on 12 August 1851 she met "The Master of my dreams". He is not a lover but her invisible protector; whomsoever he might be a fuller explanation was never provided.

Princess Bagration apparently separated from her companion either in London or somewhere on the continent. Helena Petrovna now took up with one Agardi Metrovich, the illegitimate son of the Duke of Lucca. Metrovich was a well-known opera singer, and during one of his tours he may well have become acquainted with her on a previous occasion. After staying with him for a time, probably as his mistress, she started on her peregrinations anew.

What she said occurred next is really highly improbable. She said that she made her way to Canada to study the Indians. Later she travelled in the United States and visited the Mormon settlement; in due course she said she went on to Mexico and Central America. From these places she then, according to her own account, made a brief trip to India via Ceylon. It was on this occasion she averred that made her initial attempt to visit Tibet but was unsuccessful. Returning to Europe she landed in England but on the outbreak of the Crimean War she left the country. During her sojourn in London she claimed to have met Prince Dulep Singh of Lahore, a protégé of sorts of Queen Victoria. She also seems to have been part of the entourage of Daniel Home, the spiritualist. He was very popular in society both in Britain and on the continent. Home evidently had the ability to make tables turn and to levitate. He and Helena Petrovna did not remain friends and were to become bitter enemies. At this time, and once again Sergius Witte is our source, she was to gain some acclaim as a concert pianist and to have the role of the director of the court musicians of King Milan Obrenevitch of Serbia.

After an absence of some eight years, she decided to return to

Russia and made her way to Tiflis. The Fadeyevs declined to receive her. Again, Sergius Witte is our authority when he writes that she had actually agreed to rejoin her husband. There is no truth in what he stated, indeed the situation was quite the contrary. Blavatsky was attempting to have his marriage annulled. He indicated to a friend that his wife was of no interest to him, and observed in a letter, "Time smoothes out everything, even memory." This was not to be quite the end of the story.

Seeking a refuge, she went to Pskov where she and her sister met on Christmas Day. The two women went to an estate nearby that had been bought by Vera Petrovna's late husband. At the estate she found her nephews and also her father, whose second wife had recently died. The household at Rugdevo was a comfortable enough ménage but Helena Petrovna found it somewhat boring. She indulged herself in conjuring up mischievous poltergeists to alleviate the tedium, and to show her relations that she did have occult powers. Her hostess was not overly pleased with these slightly nefarious activities, but accepted them with as good grace as she could. Apparently, Helena Petrovna's reunion with her father and her acceptable behaviour with her immediate family made a reconciliation with her grandparents possible. They invited her to stay with them in Tiflis in the summer of 1860. While there her cousin, Sergius Witte, met her and his report of her was like an earlier one, not very flattering. He described her as being exceedingly unstylish and with a somewhat dissipated appearance. However, he did note that her eyes were her best feature. "Never," he said, "in my life have I ever seen anything like that pair of eyes." The same comment was to be made of Rasputin, another "mysterious" Russian.

The final chapter of the story in the Blavatsky marriage ensued at this time. It seems there was a meeting and an attempted sort of reconciliation, but nothing came of it. The separation was to be final and permanent. One friend from her travels found himself in Tiflis, namely, Metrovich. She and he became lovers and in due course she gave birth to a son called Yuri. The child was somehow deformed and mentally subnormal. The world was told that Yuri was a "ward" and for propriety's sake the family affected to give credence to the fiction. Yuri seems to have died about the age of three in Italy and was buried under the name of Metrovich, his putative father.

For the next few years Helena Petrovna renewed her peripatetic existence. According to her own account she visited Egypt, Syria, the Balkans and Italy. She even claimed to have joined Garibaldi, and fought with his army at Mentana in 1867. She also asserted that her Master had ordered her to return to India and to make an expedition to Tibet. This story is probably highly suspect; it is more likely that she travelled with Metrovich on his concert tours.

It was on one such tour that Metrovich lost his life. He and Helena Petrovna en route to Egypt embarked on the S.S. *Eunomia*; near Alexandria there was some sort of accident – an explosion in the boiler room perhaps – and the vessel sank. Two stories of what happened have been recounted, the first being that Metrovich was drowned, the second that they both survived but shortly after arriving in Cairo Metrovich was murdered. It was rumoured that his assassin was a Roman Catholic cleric who hated Metrovich as an avowed supporter of Mazzini. Whatever the truth, Helena Petrovna found herself alone in Cairo and without any visible means of support.

With her usual ability to find a benefactor, she became acquainted with Lydia Paschkoff, a Russian explorer and early feminist, who incidentally was interested in the occult. Through her and in the company of others who shared these enthusiasms, she managed to eke out an existence. One of her new acquaintances was Emma Cutting, who provided Helena Petrovna with a home. The two women became very intimate and firm friendship ensued. This relationship was to have dire consequences for Helena Petrovna a number of years later.

In the summer of 1872, she made her last visit to Russia where she lived in Odessa. Restless as always, quarrelsome and disinclined to adapt herself to a normal existence, she decided to go to Paris in the spring of 1873. It is from this time that her saga takes on a sort of reality. Her adventures from 1849 when she left Russia for the first time read like a story written by Baron Munchausen. What is truth and what fiction is virtually impossible to ascertain. However, her place of residence in Paris can be affirmed. She lived with a cousin, Nicholas Gustavitch von Hahn, at 11 rue de l'Université. It was here that she was supposedly ordered by her Master to go to New York, and she landed in the United States in July. Her true mission can be dated from this moment, namely, 7 July 1873.

She had little money; indeed one is inclined to wonder at times how she had supported herself generally in all of her travels. If Russia was essentially a two-class society, aristocrat and peasant, New York was not too dissimilar in that there were the rich and everybody else. Helena Petrovna was very much in the latter category. She found herself a room in a sort of female commune, a non-profit co-operative at 222 Madison Avenue. Each resident had her own private accommodation, but there was a communal sitting room that was called "the office". She does not seem to have had any settled occupation, and spent much of her time in "the office" smoking constantly and entertaining her fellow residents with stories of her life. She was definitely exotic and an object of curiosity. She was friendly enough in a condescending fashion; for example, she did not permit any undue familiarity and insisted on always been addressed as "Madame".

After being in New York for several months, she was informed that her father had died and left her a modest inheritance. Evidently she had told at least some of her family where she was presently living. It took some months before this small fortune arrived, and to support herself, she found employment painting calendars and in similar activities. She also wrote occasional articles for the newspapers.

During the first year in New York she was to meet three men who were to be directly involved in her life in a variety of ways. The first was Andrew Jackson Davis, a spiritualist and a medium but not overly interested in "popular spiritualism" as such, but used her contact with the spirit world to promote his ideas on moral improvement and the general brotherhood of mankind. These ideas she was to adopt and expand in her book, *The Secret Doctrine*. Through Davis she was put in touch with Alexander Aksakov, the editor of a German journal devoted to disseminating ideas on spiritualism. In due course she was to write various articles for this periodical and to do some translation work for him. The second was Michael Constantinovitch Betanelly, a Russian businessman. He was not an intellectual but an agreeable companion being handsome and charming. The third individual was Henry Steel Olcott, a lawyer who had served in the Union army during the American Civil War rising to the rank of colonel. He wrote for the newspapers on a variety of subjects, one being on spiritualism.

He was commissioned to write a piece for *The Daily Graphic* on the Eddy brothers and their séances at their farm in Chittendon. By chance, Helena Petrovna and her friend Madame Magnon were there on the occasion of his visit. She was a very distinctive figure among the visitors. She was overweight, with hair in some disarray and wearing a bright red shirt with a voluminous black skirt and heavy boots. She smoked constantly, rolling her own cigarettes and with a tobacco pouch ready at hand. She and Olcott struck up a conversation and there was an instant rapport. He was to become a close companion when she made a life for herself in India.

While at Chittendon she indulged in a little occult activity herself by summoning up a mysterious figure from the Caucasus who was rather more interesting than the "Red Indian" familiar of the Eddy brothers. Olcott was much impressed and made her the central figure in his article for *The Daily Graphic*. This publicity enhanced her own self-esteem and also brought her some modest fame.

In the autumn of 1874, she moved to Philadelphia when she became closely associated with the business activities of Betanelly. He proposed marriage and she unwisely accepted. In so doing, she committed bigamy, as Blavatsky was still her legal husband. After only a few months the couple separated, but it may well have been a *mariage blanche*. There was a formal divorce and Betanelly returned to Russia. Her occult activities continued and via a medium she was told that one Serapis Bey of The Brotherhood of Luxor would teach her special wisdom. Olcott also was to be a pupil.

She returned to New York where she and Olcott were to share a flat and establish a sort of salon. After a time they decided to form a proper association. Henry Olcott was to be President, Helena Petrovna was named Corresponding Secretary. Among the earliest members was William Judge, later to become the leader of the American Theosophical Society. The inaugural lecture was delivered by Olcott on 17 November 1875.

For the next couple of years Helena Petrovna Blavatsky was to be much occupied in the writing of her first major literary work, *Isis Unveiled*. There is considerable controversy as to how much of the content was in any way original and to what extent she was the real author. Critics have averred that much of it was plagiarised. She herself said "the Masters" were the real source, and that she was only an amanuensis and a sort of conduit for them to get their ideas into a literary form. During the writing of the book, she allowed herself the indulgence of so-called automatic writing as if the differing orthography, literary style and turn of phrase were proof of her allegations. It is evident that she believed her own myths if others were more doubtful.

The manuscript was finally completed, but it was an inchoate mass of disconnected theories and disjointed ideas. Olcott took it to a publisher who rejected it as being too long and too incomprehensible. He was persuaded to reconsider his decision, and he gave the manuscript to an associate, Alexander Wilder, to act as editor. Wilder cut vast amounts of text, made a number of abridgements and produced a publishable corpus. Wilder does not seem to have doubted that the author had asserted the truth when she said it was all dictated to her by telepathy.

Isis Unveiled was published in the autumn of 1877. Despite the esoteric nature of the subject matter, the book received a generally good reception. Helena Petrovna seems to have been genuinely surprised at the cordial reaction to her book. *The New York Herald*'s literary critic observed that it was "one of the most remarkable productions of the century". One is temped to wonder if he were being ironical. The first printing of a thousand copies was completely sold out in ten days, which considering that it sold for seven dollars a copy made it an expensive purchase. Of course, not everybody liked the book. *The New York Times* declined to review it at all, and Daniel Douglas Home, an erstwhile friend, declared that the author was a cheat and a fraud with a scandalous private life. The public does not appear to have been in any way put off by these negative critics, and the book continued to sell and to be re-printed.

Isis Unveiled expounded a somewhat arcane set of concepts that were vaguely Middle Eastern or Indian in origin. Olcott and especially Helena Petrovna were to become associated with the Arya Somaj movement. With the appearance of *Isis Unveiled*, the Theosophical Society won new friends. For example, one was Thomas Edison and another was General Abner Doubleday who had "invented" baseball. The authoress was convinced that everything was part of a plan by her Master. She was persuaded that she and Olcott should move to India, but the latter was unconvinced. However, he was persuaded after receiving personal messages from Master Serapis and another known only as M that it was his duty to accompany her.

Prior to her leaving the United States, Helena Petrovna Blavatsky became an American citizen. It has been said by convinced adherents of theosophy that she was the first Russian woman to do so. Thomas Edison made a recording of both Olcott and Blavatsky and also of their cat Charles.

They embarked on 17 December 1878. They made a curious pair: he was the conservatively dressed author and lawyer, she the vastly fat – she weighed some 245 pounds – outrageously unfashionable female.

The trans-Atlantic crossing was quite awful for there were many storms, and seasickness was endemic. They finally landed early in January and went to London to stay with friends. During their sojourn, Helena Petrovna, much to the delight of her host and hostess, seems to have materialised a tea pot among other things and to have received a message that a secret letter would be found at Madame Tussaud's Waxworks, which it was. She herself was rather bored with these simple demonstrations of her powers, but she realised how much pleasure they gave to her friends.

In the middle of January the travellers once more boarded ship for the journey to India. This voyage was no better than the first, and Helena Petrovna was convinced that she would suffer death at sea. This was not to be her fate, and in late February they reached Bombay. Olcott kissed the quay upon landing, so pleased was he to have arrived safely. A new life was beginning for Helena Petrovna Blavatsky and Henry Olcott.

They had anticipated being made welcome by people with whom they had been in correspondence, but they were not. They stayed for a few days as guests of a local acquaintance, but soon established themselves in a "bungalow" complete with the proverbial houseboy by the name of Babula. Because Olcott and Helena Petrovna eschewed English society, the authorities were convinced that she was a Russian spy. When she made a short excursion to northern India, she was accompanied on the entire journey by a policeman.

She busied herself writing articles for various journals, and also wrote a book entitled *From the Caves and Jungles of Hindustan*. However, her main purpose in being in India was to spread the ideas of theosophy to a larger audience. To bring this about she founded a journal called *The Theosophist*. It was to have considerable success with a varied audience, who found the motto of The Theosophical Society, "There is no religion higher than truth!", much to their liking.

Alfred Sinnett, a successful journalist, and his wife both committed to the teachings of theosophy were to become close friends of Helena Petrovna Blavatsky and Henry Olcott. The Sinnetts were extremely hospitable and their friends were often asked to stay. On various occasions Helena Petrovna was to demonstrate her special powers because she knew it pleased her host and hostess.

The most famous of her "manifestations" or "materialisations" occurred on a picnic. Instead of six persons there were seven, the seventh individual being unexpected. She was challenged to do something useful with her "magic". She agreed to produce the extra teacup. Enlisting the support of Major Henderson, a police officer, she instructed him to dig at the root of a nearby tree. To the amazement of everyone but herself the teacup was found and, more astonishingly, it was of the same pattern as the other six. Just where did the teacup come from? Was it provided by Babula her houseboy, who somehow had learned there were to be a party of seven and so informed his mistress? Did the two of them arrange for the cup to be placed in a strategic place so that Major Henderson would find it as directed? We shall never know. The teacup story was to be given a wide circulation, and Helena Petrovna's special powers given greater credence.

Another of her activities was her involvement with two mahatmas, namely Koot Hoomi and another known as M. They wrote letters to various chosen recipients – M had communicated with Olcott in New York – but always through their emissary. Alfred Sinnett was one who was the recipient of their correspondence. He was to publish some of the letters he had received in his book, *The Occult World*. Alan Hume, later to be the first president of the Indian National Congress, also seems to have had dealings with the mahatmas.

The mahatmas were supposed to be members of the Brotherhood of the Snow Range and they resided in Tibet. Both Koot Hoomi and M were Hindu and the latter was Helena Petrovna's special protector. Koot Hoomi wrote almost all of his letters in French, and his English was rather second-rate. There were other mahatmas who wrote very little and there were no female mahatmas. Indeed, the mahatmas were distinctly anti-feminine, and were often critical of Helena Petrovna herself. She had a very inferior position in their world, being accepted at best as a lay sister. Her lowly status was taken as an added proof that she could not have written the letters herself. Moreover, on occasion the contents of the letters actually contradicted her stated beliefs, thus being a further indication that she was not the author but only the emissary.

In December 1882 Helena Petrovna and Henry Olcott, their houseboy Babula and Emma Cutting, her friend from Cairo days and now married to Alexis Coulomb – the couple served as housekeeper and handy man – moved to Madras. They were to acquire an elegant mansion with several outlying bungalows and dependencies. Helena Petrovna resided in the main house, Henry Olcott had his own bungalow as did the Coulombs. Babula occupied the servants' quarters. All seemed very content with the new arrangement. Various guests came to stay, among them Francis Marian Crawford, the American author. He was later to write a novel entitled *Mr Isaacs* in which comments on Anglo-Indian life and theosophy were central themes. Both Helena Petrovna and Olcott were also featured characters; they were much flattered by his amiable portray of the two of them.

The halcyon period did not last. There were attacks on the probity of Helena Petrovna, especially over the mahatmas. Anna Kingsford, the president of the London Theosophical Society, was one major critic and several prominent members of the society resigned. To re-establish her authority, Helena Petrovna decided to make a trip to London and she and Olcott left India in February 1884.

In her absence, a real crisis developed. Emma Coulomb and her husband quarrelled with the Board of Control left behind to administer the estate at Adyar. The couple were dismissed, and in their anger Emma Coulomb and her spouse declared that they could prove that the mahatma letters were in fact written by Helena Petrovna and they proceeded to do so. When Helena Petrovna learned of her former friend's actions, she felt totally betrayed, but did not herself acknowledge that the mahatmas were a fraud perpetrated by herself.

Despite the crisis engendered by Emma Coulomb, the sojourn in London was not unpleasant. The various factions in the world of theosophy seem to have agreed to differ. One group accepted Helena Petrovna's assurances about the mahatmas and they formed the so-called London Lodge. The other persons under Anna Kingsford who led the Hermetic Lodge were more independent.

The question about the mahatmas continued, and the controversy over the authorship of the letters became the basis of an article entitled, "The Collapse of Koot Hoomi", which appeared in a magazine published in Madras. The Society for Psychical Research, based in London, having initially accepted the mahatmas now began to have doubts, and they decided to investigate the Adyar community.

The society sent Richard Hodgson to discover the facts about Koot Hoomi and M. He soon became convinced that Emma Coulomb's story was true, and his report was totally damning. Hodgson managed to collect some so-called Koot Hoomi's letters which he was certain were fraudulent. The upshot was that Hodgson, who was certainly not unbiased and who believed that Helena Petrovna was a Russian agent, published an account that totally destroyed her credibility. Curiously enough almost a century later in volume fifty-three of the *Journal for Psychical Research*, there is an article by Vernon Harrison questioning the findings of Hodgson. The consequences of this article revived the debate as to whether the mahatmas ever did exist or whether they were just conjured up by Helena Petrovna for her own purposes.

She returned to India late in December 1884. One of her companions was Charles Leadbetter, a some-time Anglican clergyman and a notorious homosexual. He remained at Adyar briefly and then went on to Ceylon where he resided for many years. In due course he was to become one of the most prominent and highly influential, but certainly very suspect, persons in the world of theosophy.

The pressures on Helena Petrovna's life induced an illness that may well have been psychosomatic. The continued attacks on her by Emma Coulomb, and the report prepared by Hodgson were very damaging. Henry Olcott now intervened and taking advantage of the situation forced her to leave India in the spring of 1885. She was never to return to Adyar.

Initially she stayed in Italy but soon thereafter moved on to Würzburg in Germany. Here she began to work on a new major literary endeavour which, when finally published, appeared under the title of *The Secret Doctrine*. This book was to become the essential canon for all her true followers. Her old friend, Sinnett, came to see her and requested her permission to write her biography. She agreed but the facts were as she dictated, and the book that resulted was essentially as much fiction as fact.

Existence in Würzburg was simple and uneventful. The attacks made by Emma Coulomb more or less ceased, the report of Hodgson had little real effect as convinced theosophists rejected its findings. Her day-to-day life was made easier by the presence of Constance Wachmeister, who managed the household in an efficient manner. Olcott, who had originally engineered her departure from India, now attempted to persuade her to return. For reasons that are unclear, perhaps she felt her present situation was more conducive to completing her book, but she firmly declined his request.

Progress on the great opus continued. As with *Isis Unveiled*, the manuscript was a great mass of undigested material, and to bring it into a degree of coherence three friends undertook to edit what she had written. It was a horrendous task and took some months to complete. While her editors were at work, she moved once more, this time returning to London. Initially, she was the guest of Mabel Collins, but this domestic arrangement was not of long duration. Helena Petrovna was not an easy person; she was somewhat autocratic and self-indulgent; she dressed appallingly and was probably not overclean. Her constant smoking her hostess found disagreeable. The two women parted amicably enough, and Helena Petrovna set up her own household in the spring of 1887. At the same time, she established the Blavatsky Lodge to rival both the London and Hermetic Lodges. She arranged also for a new journal, entitled *Lucifer*, to put forward her own personal views on theosophy. She had a sort of salon receiving guests each evening, especially young people. One youthful admirer was William Butler Yeats who became convinced of her special powers and who was to retain all of his life a belief in various aspects of the occult.

The Secret Doctrine was published in 1888. There were to be two volumes of text. It was essentially an expansion of the ideas that had been the core of *Isis Unveiled*. In her new book she discussed three major ideas, namely, "that there is an omnipresent and immutable Reality of which spirit and matter are complementary aspects; secondly, that there is a universal law of periodicity, or evolution through cyclic change; and, thirdly, that all souls are identical with the universal Over soul, which is itself an aspect of the unknown Reality". Her teachings generally presented the ideas that could equate science, religion and philosophy. Theosophy was to form a society dedicated to universal brotherhood of humanity without distinction of race, colour or creed. It was to encourage the study of eastern and western ideas in a comparative manner and above all somehow "to investigate unexplained laws of nature and the hidden powers latent in man". In a very real sense, it was an epic search for the beginning of civilisation, how the universe was created, what force had fashioned it and what it all meant. Everything was in flux, "the Over soul" combines with all souls and every being experienced a number of incarnations. Two other books were to follow: *The Key to Theosophy* and *The Voice of Silence*, but these were codas to her principal work.

At this time, Helena Petrovna Blavatsky created an even more exclusive body, namely the Esoteric Section of the Blavatsky Lodge. Henry Olcott accepted the fact that there were various sections of the Theosophical Society. The principal figures being William Judge, Charles Leadbetter, Anna Kingsford, Helena Blavatsky and himself. However, as long as he was in charge at Adyar he was not unhappy.

The final chapter of Helena Petrovna Blavatsky's life was to be shared with the individual who probably became her most famous disciple, namely, Annie Besant, who had had two children while married to an Anglican clergyman, but was now a militant atheist and radical. Her first contact with theosophy was when she was asked to review *The Secret Doctrine*. Her initial reaction to what she read was highly positive and she arranged for a meeting with the author. It was a highly successful encounter. Anne Besant became almost an instant convert, but Helena Petrovna made her read Hodgson's report before accepting her into the society. Annie Besant then gave a public lecture to a large audience announcing her acceptance of theosophy. Her radical friends, such as W.T. Stead and George Bernard Shaw, were scandalised and thought she had become insane. Actually, her adherence to theosophy was to be particularly influential in her promotion of the Congress Party and Indian independence.

Anne Besant more or less took over her spiritual director's life. She moved her into her own house on Avenue Road. Despite a general decline in her health, Helena Petrovna continued her *conversaziones*. Visitors were still attracted by her ideas and personality; "the Sphinx", as she had sometimes been called, retained a mystical charm not readily explained. In the year prior to her death she was the victim of a scurrilous attack by a New York newspaper. She was declared to be a charlatan, a common thief and a woman of loose morals. It was said that she had lived in Paris for a decade with Prince Wittgenstein as her lover and had borne an illegitimate child. Her usual reaction to such charges was to decline to make any reply implying that they were not only false but also beneath contempt. On this occasion she sued the newspaper for libel. Sadly, she did not survive to learn that she had won her case, and that she had successfully refuted what had been written about her.

Early in 1891, friends found her somewhat listless, prone to depression and generally enfeebled. She died on 8 May 1891 after a short illness. Apparently, her last coherent words were "Isabel, Isabel, keep the link unbroken, do not let my last incarnation be a failure."

She had requested that after her death she be cremated. After a brief service of sorts at the crematorium in Woking her ashes were divided into three parts, one being given to Henry Olcott, one to William Judge and the third to Annie Besant. The last recipient arranged that the ashes in her possession were scattered in the Ganges. A year after her demise her closest friends and most committed devotees had a special memorial gathering. Readings from various Hindu texts were read, as were selections from her own writings. The occasion was not melancholy but rather the celebration of a life. The participants described the event as White Lotus Day. Thereafter, theosophists kept the anniversary of her demise as White Lotus Day.

The history of the theosophical movement thereafter is really a history of Annie Besant. She and Charles Leadbetter became the major figures. Henry Olcott remained in charge at Adyar until his death in 1907. Annie Besant herself moved to India immediately thereafter. In the ensuing years, the canon of Helena Petrovna Blavatsky underwent a subtle change. The principles of a universal brotherhood and the significance of Hinduism were to be replaced by a sort of oriental Christianity. This was to be particularly true with Annie Besant's proclamation that Jiddu Krishnamurti was the new messiah. His role in the theosophical world was very different to that ever envisaged by Helena Petrovna Blavatsky.

Helena Petrovna Blavatsky rejected the idea that because she was a woman she was automatically denied a role as a philosopher. She had a great vision for humanity, and was absolutely convinced of the truth of her teachings. While the mahatmas may have been essentially fraudulent, they served a useful purpose in her mission. She rejected orthodox Christianity, substituting for it a more expansive set of beliefs. God is not external but is part of every individual, and salvation comes by evolution, a process of self-realisation and repeated reincarnation. Ultimately the spirit would be liberated and return to the astral life. Helena Petrovna Blavatsky attempted the impossible, a real rapprochement between religion and science. She wanted to discern the truth of fact in an objective sense and a truth of subjective wisdom. There may be a few individuals in history such as Buddha who can convey somehow a meaning of all aspects of life but these people are rare indeed. She rejected the idea that the ultimate knowledge was science and its handmaiden technology; rather she believed that thought is reality.

In person, she was ungainly and unattractive in looks; only her eyes, as her cousin Sergius Witte had noted, had their own compelling beauty. She was autocratic, self-willed and selfish. She cared nothing for her appearance and defied convention in her dress. In company, she dominated the scene by the breadth of ideas expressed in her conversation. To gain her own ends she used people, and in particular Henry Olcott, ruthlessly. Until the end of her life, she had no doubts of her special powers. She need not have worried about her role in the great chain of being. Nobody could say that her last incarnation was a failure. Her writings continue to be read by seekers for a universal truth. The theosophical movement is alive and well, its adherents are still inspired by her teachings.

Ethel Cecilia Dodd

In late Victorian London on 22 May 1889, Lillian Dodd, the wife of John Dodd, gave birth to a daughter. The infant was christened shortly thereafter and given the names Ethel Cecilia. In due course she was to have several younger siblings. Her father had originally intended to enter the Methodist ministry, but after his marriage he abandoned the idea and became a businessman instead. The family were not overly pious; to be sure they attended the local Congregational Church, but like many people of their day they may well have done so because of social convention. There is no record of family prayers and the like.

The Dodd family did have a modest claim to celebrity. They were related to Florence Nightingale, who was Ethel Dodd's great-great-aunt. The latter on one occasion took her great-great-niece, then aged eight, to a service in St Paul's Cathedral – was it perhaps some event associated with Queen Victoria's Diamond Jubilee? Close contact between the elderly spinster – she was aged 77 at the time – was not maintained but, however, much of the intrepid character of Florence Nightingale was to be observed in the activities of her great-great-niece in later years.

While this religious service had no particular impact on the little girl, one a year later certainly did. For reasons now unknown, Ethel Dodd attended the centenary of the Church Missionary Society. Gathered in the Albert Hall were hordes of people who participated in an orgy of religious conversion. Later she was to declare that she heard a voice which ordered her to serve God and that she had reacted by an affirmative response. It is unlikely that her reply was heard by anybody, if it were uttered at all. In after years she said that from that moment, "To work for God, to win souls for Him was my only desire." This conversion of sorts gave her a sense of independence; outwardly, her life was as before.

Owing to her father's ill health, a removal from London was decreed, and the family acquired a farm in Warwickshire. Everyone flourished. Her mother, who seems to have been something of a *malade imaginaire*, became robust, her father likewise became stronger and she herself revelled in the rural life. Farm animals of all sorts were to become her companions, and animals, she discovered, had real personalities. Like many "incomers" into a village and particularly in the early twentieth century, the Dodds were not really part of the local life. They did not attend the parish church of All Saints because they were "chapel". Moreover, All Saints was "high church" and this was quite outside their own religious tradition and experience.

Of all the family, only Ethel Dodd seems to have missed her Sunday outings that had been part of her London life. Moreover, had she not at the age of nine dedicated herself to God's service, but which seemed impossible under her present circumstances. However, when she was fourteen she appears to have convinced her mother of her desire to join the Anglican Church. Her father generally disapproved, and only gave his consent in a grudging fashion. He thought this eldest daughter's enthusiasm was but a passing phase from which she would emerge a normal individual. His hopes were to be dashed in quite the reverse fashion, for she became increasingly pious. Her parents attempted to dissuade her from being confirmed, but she was determined. When asked "Why?", her response was "Because I must, don't you see!" She finally won their consent and was confirmed on 4 March 1903.

The Anglo-Catholic practices were emphasised during the confirmation classes which she had attended. One such sacrament was "penance" and as this required attendance at confession, her insistence in being fully committed incurred further parental opposition. They forbade her even to contemplate such an activity, and they made divers threats such as a removal from home and boarding school should she persist. In this instance she evidently recognised that discretion was the better part of valour and obeyed.

Despite the prohibition from full participation in church life as she would have wished, she was actively involved as much as possible. Unfortunately, at this juncture she was found to have tuberculosis, her general strength waned, and she was to become a complete invalid for over a year. Her parents, despite their opposition to her religiosity, regarded her with special affection as their eldest child, and she was given the best nursing care possible. The whole household rejoiced when and if there were signs of improvement.

Because of her illness, her schooling was of necessity interrupted. She did not permit herself the luxury of idleness, but attempted to keep up with her lessons on a regular basis. Once recovered, she resumed her special role in the family as the particular companion of her mother, assisting the latter in various domestic affairs. She also resumed her active life in the church, now accepted by her parents but still without enthusiasm.

Some three years after her confirmation, the family left the farm and moved to Leamington Spa. Here they were to reside for about half a year and it was at this time another event in Ethel Dodd's religious life occurred. While continuing to be a communicant in the Anglican Church, on one occasion she seems to have gone to confession in a Roman Catholic church. She received conditional absolution and modest penance was required. The priest commanded her to say the rosary. This experience filled her with great joy, but was not to be repeated because she was acutely aware of the disapprobation of her parents for all things that might be papistical.

Following John Dodd being offered employment in the Midlands, the family moved to Birmingham. They took up residence in a typical suburban part of the city; their new home vastly different from the farmhouse in Warwickshire. Lillian Dodd now became a real invalid. She had been much weakened by eight pregnancies and was frail. Consequently, her role in the domestic life of the household was to be much diminished, and the position was assumed almost totally by her eldest daughter. The latter coped admirably; she seemed to have revelled in her more authoritarian role in the household. It was evident that she liked being in charge, a role she was very much to enjoy in later life.

Her domestic obligations apparently did not interfere with her religious avocations. When first in Birmingham, she attended St Mary's, her local parish church, but soon transferred to St Chad's, in a less salubrious part of the city. The services at St Chad's were conducted in a fashion more to her liking. On the prompting of a friend, she took up Sunday School teaching and became a regular parish visitor as well. As if her time was not filled with domestic duties and Sunday obligations, she enrolled in a class at a local theological college in a course of study leading to a prospective career in teaching.

Never one to temper the shorn lamb from the wind in her behaviour, she began to attend daily communion services. This apparent excessive piety caused an uproar with much parental displeasure expressed. What they did not know was that at St Chad's she went to confession. Had they been told their anger would have had no bounds. This disobedience to her mother and father does not seem to have disturbed her unduly. In this instance, as in others later, she believed that what she was doing was right. Moreover, she had no doubts but that it was

God's will and as such a more than proper enough reason for her actions.

Chance, or perhaps, as she would have observed, God, inspired her to attend the services at St Jude's, another Anglican church rather than St Chad's. Part of the congregation at St Jude's were a group of nuns. Ethel Dodd had not hitherto known that in the Church of England there were any such sisterhoods. They were not numerous, and, indeed, in Birmingham there was only one community. She was much impressed by the service at St Jude's and the presence of the sisters. The latter were members of the Society of the Precious Blood founded in 1905. Knowing little or nothing about their work, she wrote to the Mother Superior, Mother Millicent Mary, asking for information. She was now eighteen and determined to lead her own life. Following a satisfactory reply to her letter, she decided that possibly she had a "vocation". She made arrangements to meet the Reverend Mother, and received an invitation to spend a week with the sisters.

When confronted with this news, the reaction of her parents can only be imagined. They were totally opposed to the plan, but their reaction did nothing to alter their daughter's determination. One wonders what might have been her reaction if they had appealed to her sense of obligation to the family generally, and, in particular, to the need to care for her mother. Curiously enough there is no evidence that they acted in this way; their opposition was, as in the past, that her behaviour was to them irrational. For these two months prior to her betaking herself to 51 John Bright Street where the sisters resided, her life at home was difficult. However, she was careful not to show any sign of hostility to her parents or to her brothers and sisters. Finally the day came: on 6 January, the Feast of the Epiphany, she left her parents' house for what in due course would be a new life.

On arrival at the convent, she was instantly impressed by the way of life as lived by the sisters. She was aware of its general austerity; its lack of domestic facilities, and she knew that personal intimacy was not encouraged. By the end of the week, Ethel Dodd knew that she had a "vocation", and she asked Mother Millicent Mary if she could join the community. The older woman agreed. Her parents predictably disagreed. She was under age, and they formally forbade her from taking the step which she aspired to make. For the next twelve months parental authority prevailed. To alleviate her sense of frustration, she managed to get part-time teaching positions, and also acted as a coach for boys wishing to be wireless telegraphers in the civil service. These activities had the approbation of her parents.

After the year passed, she was finally of age and could make her own decision. On 7 December, St Ambrose Day, she prepared herself to leave home. She was about to fulfil her destiny as she saw it. She declared: "let's be happy, let me be happy today!" These brief remarks she observed to the family dog and to all and sundry. Her father alone could not bear to see her depart, and left for his office early. As she drove away in a cab, she turned to see her mother and her siblings in floods of tears; for a moment she had regrets, but these feelings were suppressed. Once inside the convent she was "home". Her reception was formal. The first night a bed was made up for her in the laundry, no cell being immediately available, and it was to be in the laundry where she was to work to learn obedience. In a sense, the initial sojourn in a convent or monastery is not unlike the earliest days in the army where rough and ready training demands a complete acceptance of authority.

For some three months Ethel Dodd worked in the laundry, when it was noted that she was unwell she was promoted to pantry duty, she served in the dining room, the kitchen and the scullery. Once again, she collapsed. Convent discipline was all very well, but the demands made upon the young postulant were unrealistic and almost cruel. Ethel Dodd was determined, however, not to be defeated. As a form of relief, she was required to assist a sister in a mission house but the funds available to supply food for the two of them were inadequate. Near starvation ensued. This state of affairs brought an intervention by her parents. They had acquiesced, albeit reluctantly, to her life in the convent and tried anew to prevent her from taking vows to become a full-fledged novice. Once again, she insisted on the correctness of her decision, and her parents could do nothing to change her mind.

She became a full member of the community, clothed in her habit and with the name of Cecilia Mary. Ethel Dodd as such no longer existed. Her existence henceforth was as a religious. All was not as she had hoped, however. There was a plan that the Society of the Precious Blood should become a totally enclosed order. This idea did not appeal: for Cecilia Mary the life of a nun was service not just prayer. Rather than undergo total enclosure, she arranged to transfer to another order, namely, the Society of the Incarnation of the Eternal Son. Her leave-taking of Mother Millicent Mary was sad, but Cecilia Mary had learned much from this redoubtable woman in the twenty-one months under her leadership. Many of the lessons she herself was to impose on postulants and novices in the future.

The new sisterhood was Franciscan, and, much to her surprise, was less rigorous than her previous life. This was not entirely pleasing to her as she almost revelled in a state of physical and mental hardship. Indeed, life was almost too comfortable. In her new situation she participated in parish visiting and in the management of three orphanages. The latter she was to liken with her experience at home with her brothers and sisters.

At this juncture, her father decided that he, his wife and the children should move to Canada. It was assumed that life in "the colonies" would bring a better and more prosperous existence. This was the stated reason, but also John Dodd was determined to prevent his youngest daughter, who greatly admired her eldest sister, from adopting a similar way of life. She who had abandoned her family now felt abandoned by them.

Cecilia was not inclined to mope; the sisters were her family, and she devoted herself to the community. The nuns were busily involved in attempting to alleviate the misery of many of the citizens in Birmingham. The very poor had only charity or the workhouse, but the outbreak of war in the summer of 1914 was to bring demands on society which had never previously been anticipated.

During the war, the sisters of the Society of the Incarnation of the Eternal Son performed many tasks. They did much parish visiting, worked in hospitals, hostels and orphanages. They helped to comfort the bereaved families whose husbands and sons were killed in France. It can be said without any form of contradiction that they filled a role that probably no other group could do.

Twenty-five years after her birth and half a decade as a postulant and novice, Cecilia Mary became a full sister. It was for her a great occasion. She gave her vow to serve God for the rest of her life. She received the veil from the bishop as the sign of purity and modesty; from him also she received the ring which formally made her the bride of Christ. In her new role, she assumed a greater responsibility. The sisters had been in charge of several orphanages; she found then badly administered and in debt. With her general efficiency she managed to persuade some more affluent people in Birmingham to come to her assistance. The upshot was that after less than a year under her direction these institutions were completely solvent.

Cecilia assumed that the pattern of her life was now established but fate intervened. Her father wrote and told her that her mother had a fatal illness. To help her family at this juncture she asked her superior for permission to go to Canada for a few months. Permission was granted and in May 1919 she sailed from England for Montreal.

The trans-Atlantic journey took some ten days and the trans-Canada railway trip at least five. Cecilia knew nothing about Canada, but her education was about to begin.

When she was met in Vancouver, she found a family not quite as she had imagined. Her mother was not dying, frail yes but improved; her father had a good and rewarding job with the Canadian Pacific Railway; her siblings had varied lives – one brother had been killed during the war, another was still recovering from wounds, a third had full employment, and her sisters, too, were part of the new world. It was clear that she was not an essential element of the Dodd existence.

While unable to live a communal life, for there were no Anglican sisters in British Columbia, she assiduously attended St James's whose rector told her that he very much wished there were sisters to help with parish life. In due course she met the Archbishop of New Westminster, Adam de Poncier, and he too expressed similar sentiments, but she was totally unwilling at this juncture to abandon her order and remain in Vancouver.

She was, however, in a quandary. She wondered if she had made a mistake in leaving her original community; she wrote to Mother Millicent Mary proposing to rejoin the Society of the Precious Blood. Mother Millicent Mary apparently replied in the affirmative welcoming "the lost sheep" to the fold. However, the reverend mother superior of the Society of the Incarnation of the Eternal Son rejected the idea outright, and demanded Sister Cecilia return to England. Archbishop de Poncier now took a hand and he wrote to Mother Gertrude Clare asking her to release Sister Cecilia for work in Canada. This request was also denied. Sister Cecilia had come to see that she could be of very real use in Canada, but it seemed as if this was not to be.

Dutifully, she returned to England but was not happy. She was aware that Mother Gertrude Clare was implacably opposed to any change in her situation. As usual when Cecilia wanted something, she was convinced that her wishes had divine approbation. Aware that she could appeal to the community as a whole for permission to leave the order, she decided to do so. Somewhat surprisingly they agreed – perhaps they sensibly felt that a dissatisfied member in their midst was hardly conducive to harmony. Cecilia could return to Canada; her father sent her passage money. Rather spitefully the order reclaimed part of it, but it did not much matter. Sister Cecilia arrived in Canada in 1922, aged 32 years. A new life lay ahead.

An observer might note that Sister Cecilia Mary had twice accepted obedience to an order and to a mother superior, but for reasons of her own had withdrawn the oaths that she had given. For the next 67 years of her life she was to be in charge of her destiny. Not for nothing was she a great-great-niece of Florence Nightingale.

Upon her arrival in Vancouver she was in the unique position of being the only Anglican nun in the city, or indeed in the province of British Columbia. Although welcomed by Archbishop de Poncier, she was financially dependent on her father. To provide herself with status, Sister Cecilia Mary proceeded to establish her own order to which she gave the name The Society of the Love of Jesus. The rule was Benedictine; previously she had been under the Augustinian and Franciscan rules. It could not be a surprise to anybody that Sister Cecilia became the Mother Superior. For the moment Mother Cecilia was the only full member; she had recruited another young woman as a postulant, but she was very much on probation.

Mother Cecilia and her colleague rented a modest house – the rent was paid by her mother – which was named St Anthony's House. The place was furnished with items given by the neighbours and other sympathetic people. To support the establishment, Mother Cecilia decided to open a hostel for the children of working mothers. The project was given some publicity by the local newspapers – an Anglican nun was news. Very quickly there were many applications for places. The original house was too small but, nothing daunted and without adequate funding, a bigger place was rented. The hostel formally opened in September 1922, some five months after the Society of the Love of Jesus had been founded. Nearly fifty children were at St Anthony's House by Christmas.

Nothing succeeds like success. Reports of the activities of Mother Cecilia reached various sisterhoods and some of these nuns left their orders to come to Vancouver. The community also attracted a number of potential postulants. Not satisfied with the physical care of young children, Mother Cecilia decided to open a school. Initially, only the primary classes were organised but this was to be modified over the years with older pupils receiving instruction. Once again the project of Mother Cecilia outgrew its physical situation.

Rather than pay rent for a building, Mother Cecilia took a gamble and with borrowed funds bought some land, and supervised the erection of a school building. This new institution, named St Anthony's College, like the hostel, was soon over-subscribed and with some 200 girls enrolled, about one third of them boarders. Mother Cecilia engaged a university graduate, Sister Mary Louise, to act as headmistress and other professional staff were employed. Mother Cecilia herself taught religious knowledge to the pupils.

Within the community Mother Cecilia was the guiding figure. There were no rivals to challenge her authority. The school gained wide fame because of its academic excellence. In addition the school and the hostel, Mother Cecilia had set up a residential home for elderly people. All of these activities gained for her the respect and affection of the city of Vancouver; she was a public figure in every sense of the word.

Quite unexpectedly Mother Cecilia once more behaved in a somewhat astonishing fashion. She seems to have become convinced that her religious vocation was incomplete and that she and the community should join the Roman Catholic Church. The Anglicans were very distressed by this decision, none more so than Archbishop de Poncier. Naturally his Roman Catholic opposite number, Archbishop William Duke was exultant. By some act of legerdemain, Mother Cecilia managed to retain all of the assets of the previous Anglican community. Archbishop Duke was unaware of the tenacity of will of his new convert and when he attempted to assert episcopal control over the erstwhile Anglicans, he found himself thwarted. Mother Cecilia determined to go her own way; she appealed to Cardinal Pacelli, later Pope Pius XII, asking that the former rule and habit be retained. Rome agreed. Archbishop Duke was furious, but there was little that he could do.

He did manage to insist that St Anthony's College become essentially a Roman Catholic institution. Mother Cecilia objected as few of the pupils, and practically none of the staff, were Roman Catholics, but her episcopal superior was adamant. Mother Cecilia, who actually owned the building and land used by the school, decided to close the place, lest it lose its good academic reputation. What to do with the buildings? She decided to extend the housing for elderly and infirm people that she had established earlier.

Mother Cecilia had never experienced any real sense of control by Archbishop de Poncier, but things under Archbishop Duke were soon to be different. Initially, Mother Cecilia and the nuns were occupied with remaking the former school into a priory and guesthouse. There was a formal opening early in 1939. It should be noted that the new establishment catered to the more affluent, with the indigent housed in less elegant quarters. Relations between Mother Cecilia and the Archbishop went from bad to worse. A new spiritual director, a Jesuit, was appointed, and he was openly hostile to the activities of Mother Cecilia. She was determined that the archbishop and his minions should not destroy all her work and she applied to Rome again. Once more Pacelli, now the Pope, supported her independence. The whole of the Vancouver archdiocese was outraged, but there was nothing they could do. Mother Cecilia then took a further independent course of action. Owning all of the buildings of the priory herself – she had carefully ensured that they were in her name – Mother Cecilia sold the entire operation to the government for $100,000. Following this coup she quickly bought a hundred-room hotel in Victoria outside the jurisdiction of Archbishop Duke. Requesting permission to take up residence on Vancouver Island, Mother Cecilia managed to escape from episcopal authority she found odious. Sensibly Archbishop Duke agreed; probably he was not unhappy to rid himself of the umbrageous Mother Cecilia. The latter, adept at managing the press, managed to have the whole affair reported in the most favourable light.

The residential hotel was a great success, as had been the previous establishment in Vancouver. The sisters initially resided in the hotel, but this was not a happy arrangement. Mother Cecilia, adroit in real-estate speculation, bought another house for the sisters which was more satisfactory and appropriate. In 1945, she bought a second hotel which prospered as well. Other property was acquired too, all of which seemed to reinforce her business acumen and to guarantee her power. Her successes seemed to ensure that she could face no real challenge to her authority and control of the Society of the Love of Jesus. If success in the business and commercial worlds were any indication of salvation, as assumed in certain Calvinistic circles, it was evident that Mother Cecilia had a direct passport.

In 1951 Mother Cecilia moved her community to a more rural situation. She had acquired some nine acres of land, and she intended to erect a more elegant and agreeable residence for elderly and infirm people. She disposed of her real estate holdings in Victoria, retaining only for the moment the smaller of her residential hotels, which was very profitable and place it under the management of one of her brothers. The new acquisition was to be given the name of St Mary's Priory.

The difficulties with Archbishop Duke were not initially repeated in Victoria. James Hill, her ecclesiastical superior, was not confrontational and he permitted Mother Cecilia a large degree of independence. Some of the local Roman Catholic clergy were rather less than enthusiastic and regarded her and her colleagues with modified rapture. Perhaps her own feelings may well be seen in respect to her business activities: "I was careful never to let the Church have anything to do with it and I certainly wouldn't let the Bishop see the books!"

In 1961 Mother Cecilia retired as head of the order, a new Superior Sister, Mary Ursula, was elected to replace her in November. Mother Cecilia had a new project, namely, to establish an animal rescue establishment. Bishop Hill does not appear to have opposed the idea. The Priory flourished and the animal centre would keep Mother Cecilia occupied. All might have been as he hoped had he survived, for he was a tactful individual who generally managed Mother Cecilia with considerable adroitness. Unfortunately, Bishop Hill died in the spring of 1962.

In late 1962 a new player arrived on the scene. The Vatican named a young progressive, idealistic reformer, Remi de Roo, as bishop. He was less sympathetic to Mother Cecilia and her continued activities in animal welfare. He was to be much irritated when she wrote to Rome proposing that her successor as Mother Superior should be replaced for reasons not specified, possibly because she felt that funds properly ought to be spent on the residents of St Mary's priory rather than on the various animals under Mother Cecilia's care. On this occasion Rome was to be unsympathetic and de Roo, on learning of her letter, which incidentally was sent to him, was naturally displeased. Once again Mother Cecilia was acting without diocesan authority. The matter was to get out of hand. Father Keber, the Apostolic Vicar to the Society of the Love of Jesus, came to the conclusion the animal shelter should be closed. Mother Cecilia declined to accept his advice, and supposedly told him that rather than give up the animals, she was prepared to risk excommunication.

On 2 March 1965 Rome took a hand. Mother Cecilia was ordered to amalgamate her order with some other Benedictine community, that the animal shelter should be closed forthwith and she and her associates return to Mount St Mary's Priory. Father Keber hoped that the whole business could be settled decently and quietly. He was quite mistaken in this hope. Mother Cecilia had no intention of submitting to papal authority in this instance. Indeed, any person who had even a remote understanding of her character and past history would have been aware how intransigent she could be when thwarted. Throughout her entire life she was always convinced of the rightness of her actions despite any opinions to the contrary. Father Keber now ordered the sisters at the shelter to return to the priory immediately.

Mother Cecilia's reaction was not what Father Keber anticipated. She called on the public to support her cause. In an interview with the press she declared that the Good Shepherd Shelter was to be a private charity not under the direction of the Roman Catholic Church. Further, she said that she and the sisters at the shelter would continue to work there. Bishop de Roo had a rebellion on his hands, and it provided very unfortunate publicity for him. The local community was on the side of Mother Cecilia and donations of money from varied sources were sent to help provide the funds to maintain the shelter. Animal welfare was a popular cause. On the occasion of a further meeting with reporters she took special care to make it known that she and her colleagues were probably the first nuns to be fully involved in such activities.

Bishop de Roo may have lost the first round, but was not defeated. Acting on Mother Cecilia's request in her letter to Rome, he proceeded to acquiesce; he, too, had a few tricks up his sleeve. A meeting was convened; two sisters from the United States were admitted to the community by a vote. In the ensuing election one of the two interlopers was chosen as prioress by a small majority. As a consequence Mother Cecilia and her intimates were no longer players of any significance at the priory.

Undismayed by these events, Mother Cecilia focused all of her attention on the animal shelter. Her wish to extend its activities were rejected by the local planning body with the result that she decided to move to a more rural site. She proceeded to sell the property and with her usual business acumen made a profit on her original investment. She bought considerable acreage with the money in hand. Simultaneously, she stated that the Society of the Love of Jesus was now under the protection of the Old Catholic Church. She averred that she and the sisters associated with her were still "Catholic" but free from the jurisdiction of Bishop de Roo.

The new animal shelter was organised and controlled by Mother Cecilia; some seven sisters had joined her in this new endeavour. A schism of sorts ensued shortly when two sisters defected and returned to the Priory and submitted to Bishop de Roo's authority. The two defectors accused Mother Cecilia of loving money and power to the detriment of all else. In a sense, though, it could be said that there was now a truce of sorts between the bishop and Mother Cecilia.

In 1971, some half dozen years after the move to Mill Bay a fire seriously damaged a number of kennels and stables. Mother Cecilia did not lack for friends. The boys from Brentwood College assisted in cleaning the mess and caring for the animals. News of the fire was reported widely by the press and substantial donations of money came from all over Canada and the United States. Contributions were also sent from the British Isles, where it is well known that dogs and other animals have a high priority in national sentiment.

By 1973 Mother Cecilia seems to have abandoned the Old Catholic Church and to have returned to the Anglican Communion. Bishop de Roo formally excommunicated her and those intimately associated with her. Ownership of St Mary's Priory was still in dispute and a legal case of some seven months was needed to resolve the question. The judiciary was now to have the experience of coping with Mother Cecilia. One senior judge allegedly observed of her, "A most difficult Lady to deal with!" This might well be said to be one of the great understatements of the day. The final judgement stated that Mother Cecilia had no claim to the property at Colwood. Bishop de Roo had won; ultimately St Mary's Priory was sold for about one and a half million dollars.

(Ironically, some of the money was to be invested in due course by Bishop de Roo in acquiring a stable of Arab racehorses, an investment that failed miserably. Mother Cecilia was never to know how the money had been spent, but if she had she might well have been in full approbation of the project.)

Mother Cecilia did not fade away into obscurity. In 1974 a documentary film was made about her and the animal shelter, which attracted considerable attention. A year later she was to appear on television giving her side of her activities and castigating Bishop de Roo and his allies. The Good Shepherd Animal Shelter was formally organised as a private charity with Mother Cecilia as president. Financially, despite generous donations, the whole operation was not really viable. However, Mother Cecilia seems to have convinced at least one bank manager to lend her ten thousand dollars to tide over the immediate liabilities.

Although now nearly ninety years old, she continued to be actively involved with the shelter on a daily basis. Rising at six in the morning and after attending a daily religious service she made a tour of inspection of the various animals under her charge. In fact, on her ninetieth birthday, she personally noted there were 24 horses, 80 dogs, 4 donkeys, numerous cats and many birds living at the shelter. She augmented funds by selling a monthly journal called *The Shepherd's Crook* which she edited. Incidentally, she also had a business making coffins for deceased pets.

Anni domini gradually took over her life. Wistfully she is reported to have said, "There is so much to do, very much to do, if only I were twenty-five years younger. . . ." She celebrated her ninety-sixth birthday in great style but her dearest friend, Sister Mary Julia, acknowledged privately that the shelter was in deep financial troubles owing some one hundred thousand dollars, despite gifts of over fifty thousand dollars annually from the public. The once-friendly bank managers were calling for repayment.

Ill health forced her to leave the Shelter of the Good Shepherd. She moved to a hospital near Victoria which was called Juan de Fuca. Ironically, this hospital was the former St Mary's Priory, which the government had bought from Bishop de Roo. Mother Cecilia, instead of being in charge, was merely one of the aged residents.

Mother Cecilia finally expired in her centenary year on 22 Mary 1989. After all of her battles with the Roman Catholic hierarchy, she had made her peace with the church and died a communicant. Bishop de Roo permitted prayers to be said on her behalf and a requiem mass took place at the Holy Rosary Church near the erstwhile St Mary's Priory.

Her last years had been remarkably peaceful. She had led a limited existence as the aged invalid. The Shelter would die with her – she was its creator, its guiding spirit and without her direction it could not survive. She had avowed that animals had the same right to life as human beings. While she did not aver that animals had souls, she observed: "We do not believe that an animal has a human soul, perhaps it is wrong to say that an animal has a soul at all, or a man for that matter. Perhaps it would be correct to say that animals and men *are* souls – souls embodied." No animal placed in her care as long as it was healthy was ever put down.

The local newspaper noted at her passing, "To this day we're not quite sure what Mother Cecilia was all about – but she was joyfully alive, undoubtedly caring, delightfully unpredictable and eminently worth knowing." She had gone her own way defying parents, her superiors in convents, bishops of the Anglican, Roman Catholic and Old Catholic churches, neighbours and public authorities. She might well be thought outrageous, impudent and impulsive but like most reformers convinced of the rightness of all that she did. As noted earlier, there was much of the spirit and determination of her great-great-aunt, Florence Nightingale.

Perhaps what was said of St Margaret of Scotland might well sum up Mother Cecilia and serve as her epitaph: "She united so much strictness with her sweetness of temper, such great pleasantries with her severity that all who waited up on her loved her, while they feared her in fearing loved her!"

Aimée Semple Macpherson

Rural Canada in the late Victorian age would seem a curious birthplace for one of the twentieth century's most significant religious revivalists and foundress of an extremely successful Pentecostal church. Aimée Elizabeth Kennedy, better known in history by the name of Aimée Semple Macpherson, was born in the province of Ontario on 9 October 1890. She was the only child of a somewhat curious marital situation. Her mother Minnie was only fifteen years of age when she married James Kennedy, who was thirty-five years her senior. The youthful bride had been part of his household as a domestic who looked after his invalid wife. Upon the latter's demise, and in order to silence any local gossip if she continued to live in his house, Minnie and James went to the United States and were married very quietly.

James Kennedy was a cautious, conservative and frugal person, a Methodist and traditional in his outlook on matters both secular and sacred. His youthful bride was an outgoing, gregarious individual. In contrast to her husband, she was a member of the Salvation Army, very actively involved in all of its aspects not only as a preacher but also in the administration of its Sunday school.

When their daughter was born, her mother was determined from the moment of the infant's birth that she would become a child of the Salvation Army. To the more respectable citizenry, the Army was a hysterical, noisy, boisterous and rather unsound religious institution. There were no clergy, no ritual, there was singing of tuneful hymns, personal testimony and lengthy sermons; the Salvationists regarded themselves as the soldiers of the Lord. All persons male or female were equal. Little Aimée Kennedy was to be very much part of this organisation; the orthodox traditions of her father's Methodism played only a minor role.

By the age of four, she was a regular attendant of the Salvation Army Sunday School, and here she was introduced to bible stories. Indeed, in later years people were often impressed by her biblical knowledge, and she always asserted that it came from her early association with Sunday school.

If she enjoyed her life with the Salvation Army, it cannot be said that initially she much liked secular schooling. Apparently she was a somewhat indifferent and rebellious pupil. This was to change when she was to be enrolled at Ingersoll Collegiate Institute. She was challenged by her studies and her teachers, with the result that she was a changed person. Academically she was to become something of a prodigy. Another aspect of her life that emerged at this time was her discovery of real thespian talents. She was encouraged by various church groups and others to participate in the entertainment at local festivities. She became quite professional in presenting monologues and comic songs on these occasions. In other circles she might have been encouraged to become an actress, but in rural Ontario the theatre as such was the devil's church and all actresses were scarlet women. Aimée Semple Macpherson was to admit in later years that she had much enjoyed the applause her appearances received.

Her idyllic and innocent world was threatened when, for a time, and as a result of reading a book on Darwinian evolution, she briefly lost her religious faith. With the enthusiasm of a convert, she became an agnostic, but her new-found zeal did not seem to make her happy. She recollected the biblical text, "For what shall it profit a man if he gain the whole world and lose his own soul." She felt abandoned and alone, re-conversion was painful. Revelation was to come through the efforts of a young missioner and preacher, Robert Semple. He became the agent of her conversion. His preaching at Pentecostal meeting was inspirational. God spoke through him and she was to renew her child-like faith, the world of rationalism was totally abandoned. Six months after her spiritual re-discovery, she and Robert Semple were married on 12 August 1908. They made a charming and attractive couple. They moved to Chicago where on 2 January 1909 Robert Semple was ordained a pastor of the Full Gospel Assembly. The youthful minister and his wife preached and worked in various missions. They were a team and as a team they were to embark on a joint missionary experience. Fate had destined them for a calling to Hong Kong.

Early in the spring, they left the United States travelling first for England and then on to Belfast. They went to stay in a village where Robert Semple was born. Their sojourn was brief, but in retrospect it might well have been the happiest period of her life. The countryside was magical, she and Robert were in love; that was sufficient. They returned to England and stayed in London as the guests of a wealthy Pentecostalist. He arranged for young Aimée Semple to preach in the Albert Hall despite the fact that she had never faced a large audience. Her sermon, according to her own report, was extemporaneous and the listeners were apparently much moved. Without knowing, Aimée Semple had found her metier.

The missionary and his wife arrived in Hong Kong in June 1910. There was a heat wave. Aimée Semple was exhausted, but aware that she had to cope with all adversities and managed to do. Robert Semple threw himself into his new duties, preaching daily. Malaria struck them both. He died on 17 August 1910; a month later to the day her daughter, Roberta Starr Semple, was born. What was to be the fate of the youthful mother with an infant in a strange and alien land, without friends or money?

Her mother, Minnie Kennedy, rescued her, sending funds for the return passage and generous and unexpected benefactors ensured her survival until her departure. Mother, daughter and grandchild were to be reunited in New York. Initially Minnie Kennedy had assumed that all three would live together, but this was not a happy arrangement. After a short stay, Aimée Semple went to Chicago. This, too, was not overly agreeable and in desperation she returned to Ingersoll and her father's farm. Very quickly she found this existence limiting also, and decided once again to try life in New York. She had not been idle; she helped in various Pentecostal missions singing hymns, praying with converts and bearing witness. Back in New York she became acquainted with Harold Stuart Macpherson – better known as "Mack" – and early in 1912 they were married. There was to be yet another move, this time to Providence, Rhode Island.

Aimée Semple Macpherson was to remember the next three years as the most dismal time of her life. She found it tedious just to be a wife, a mother – her son Rolf was born in 1913 – and a homemaker, dreary and boring. In reality, it was not at all disagreeable, but it simply was not the life she wished to lead. She felt she must escape. An inner voice suggested the way: she felt she was commanded to resume her religious vocation and go to preach "the good news". Surely, the world of the evangelist would be more exciting than the dullness of domesticity in Providence. Initially, she did not heed the inner voice, even though it was telling her what she wanted to do. She became ill, surgery was required, and she was not expected to survive, but like her sudden conversion by Robert Semple, she made a miraculous recovery. In the spring of 1915, she left her husband and, taking her children with her, once more returned to the family farm. From here a new world was to unfold.

Leaving her children with their grandmother, Minnie Kennedy, who also had rejoined her husband, Aimée Semple Macpherson went off to a Pentecostalist camp meeting in Kitchener, Ontario. Before departing, she sent a message to her husband in Providence suggesting that he join her in her new life. He made no immediate reply. The camp meeting was to see her in her public persona, namely as an evangelist. She was imbued with the spirit, the inner voice spoke to her and she was inspired. Through her preaching she was to captivate her audience as she had in London. This time their reaction was to be more overt – speaking in tongues, wild paroxysms of physical activity, tears and groans – the preacher worked on those who heard her like a hallucinogenic drug. She was now fully in the Pentecostal tradition, she was the handmaiden of God; thereafter she would never knowingly deviate from what she saw as her mission.

From the very inception of her evangelical career she was prepared to use any and all methods to save souls. She recognised that theatrical excesses in the eyes of some were but the rituals of others. She went into the streets calling on sinners to follow her and, somehow, as if by magic she succeeded. A woman preacher was somewhat novel; there was a sense of glamour that she brought to the pulpit as she was very attractive. The local rural people responded to her message. Later in 1915, she was to organise her own personal service in a marquee. It was to be the first of a great sequence that was ultimately to lead to the erection of the Angelus Temple in Los Angeles. She had become aware that the masses were not directed necessarily by reason but often by passion. The great leader or the great evangelist directs this passion into the route deemed the most desirable. In this instance she was convinced that she was leading people on the road to salvation. Not everyone was attracted by her preaching; some hoodlums who despised these religious out-pourings attacked the camp meetings; local worthies found it all too excessive and had her arrested for disturbing the peace. Undismayed by the hostility she continued on her mission. Harold Macpherson had finally responded to her appeal and he joined the crusade. The way was seemingly clear for her to fulfil her destiny.

From 1915 until her death nearly three decades later, Aimée Semple Macpherson was to gain renown as a great preacher. In early days the tours were seemingly directed by whim as she made her way from New England to the South and ultimately from East to West in the United States and to Canada, Europe, the Antipodes and Asia. She was to preach to black and white, to Orientals or whomever, be they the elite or the commonality. She had a charisma that overcame natural inhibitions and transformed the lives of many persons. Her sermons, even when reread decades after they were delivered, show a very deep sense of personal commitment. Traditionalists often believed that somehow she hypnotised her congregations, that she took possession of them in a diabolic sense but her traducers were not infrequently confounded when her influenced continued undiminished after she had moved to another venue.

It was at this juncture in her career that she became directly involved in healing. Her first recorded success was with a young woman who was a cripple. As a consequence of the evangelist's prayers and touch she was healed. This event was to lead to many similar occasions. For her it was the sign of the validity of Hebrews 13:8: "Jesus Christ is the same yesterday, today and forever". He could heal the sick and the maimed; by His power and through his mediatrix the same could be done in the first decades of the twentieth century. Aimée Semple Macpherson was convinced that such powers came directly from Christ and that she played little or no personal role.

Her camp meetings occupied her for the next three years. She had bought a car and it became the symbol of her mission, a church on wheels. Crowds gathered wherever and whenever she chose to set up her tent. Her mother made a quick visit to Florida to note her daughter's success. She observed that, despite the presence of Mack, the whole operation was very disorganised. She was, however, able to give her approbation to her daughter's wardrobe, namely, the simple white dress, the virginal bride of Christ. The tent encampments were to enlarge Aimée Semple Macpherson's experience with crowds and the need to keep a sense of control. She used hymns, dramatic improvisations, known as "illustrated sermons", to ensure that her audience's attention was centred on her and on her alone.

The way of life of the Macphersons can only be described as "gypsy". In a sense they were not unlike "new age travellers" but with a difference in that their peregrinations had a special purpose. Mack finally came to the conclusion that this form of existence was for him unsatisfactory; at best he was only "an attendant lord". After a series of somewhat acrimonious discussions, the couple separated. There was to be no reconciliation. He went back to Providence and lived a more settled existence. He and his wife were ultimately to be divorced. Minnie Kennedy joined the entourage. She and her daughter and the latter's family were to be closely associated for a couple of decades.

Aimée's life was one of sermons, camp meetings; her message was simple, direct and egalitarian. Salvation was possible for all; it was not a special privilege for a select few. Belief, repentance and reception of the Holy Spirit guaranteed the destruction of original sin through conversion.

The summer of 1918 saw Aimée Semple Macpherson on her high road to fame. The assemblage was on the grand scale with kitchens, lavatories, sleeping tents, but the focal point was her gospel tent. Here she delivered sermons several times a day, by the end of the week she had a congregation of some ten thousand. All-night services were organised, she called on other evangelists to join her mission. This revival lasted for several weeks, followed by tours of New England and New York. Minnie Kennedy took charge of the arrangements for there were to be no more spontaneous and seemingly directionless endeavours. Moreover, it was at this time that Aimée Semple Macpherson took the costume that was to be her uniform: she was to wear a simple white dress and over it a military cape. She was to be seen as the Florence Nightingale of God's army.

Later that year she, her mother and her children drove to the west coast. This was a very considerable feat as the super-highways of today did not then exist and cars were much inferior also. The journey of some 4000 miles was completed by December. She began her mission services in Los Angeles almost immediately, and within days she was filling a large auditorium, which easily seated over three thousand people. Los Angeles welcomed her, nay, more, the city and its denizens fell in love with her. Funds were collected to purchase a house for the local population were determined to keep their mediatrix with God in the city. Initially her attraction was the evangelist's power of healing. For three years until 1922 she led over 30 revivals. The press took notice of her, and rapidly she gained more fame than any film star or politician of the day. In an age before television, and with radio in its infancy, the newspaper was the conduit to the public. Aimée knew her public and the journalists ensured that they were kept abreast of her activities.

The "healing services" were exhausting, but she could not cease these performances because the congregations to whom she preached would not allow it. No performer in any of the dramatic arts ever had such an audience. Aimée Semple Macpherson seemed able to evoke the holy presence, and the converted almost believed that they saw Christ Himself. She continued to disavow that these powers were in any way personal, but the crowds were convinced otherwise. Her son, Rolf Macpherson, later was to see it initially as a manifestation of the age. Faith healing overcame the failures of contemporary medicine. Science had not yet acquired the universal authority of the late twentieth century.

Upon her return to her house in Hollywood, she envisaged a more permanent site for her religious activities. To raise the necessary funds for the construction of the church, she had to make yet another tour. Not only were there camp meetings, but she delivered sermons on the radio too. Money was needed and donors were persuaded by utilising all of the arts of the advertising moguls. Potential benefactors bought miniature bags of cement, tiny chairs and other such items and they contributed over £100,000. The widow's mite and the banker's gold were given an equally warm reception. She gained the support of one gypsy family or clan whose king she had cured by her healing service. They were to contribute directly to the Angelus Temple by paying for the so-called Calvary stained-glass window, which had pride of place in the building.

The revival in Denver brought in £40,000. She was to have a peculiar adventure in the city: apparently she was kidnapped by the Ku Klux Klan who wished her no harm, but merely wanted to convey to her their approbation of her activities. It is unclear why they could not have done so in a less flamboyant fashion. Later two hooded figures were to bring her a large bag filled with money. She was never to have contact with the Klan again and the whole thing remains something of a mystery.

To regain her strength after such strenuous activities, she took a lengthy sea voyage to Australia. En route she wrote sermons for the mission in the Antipodes, prepared articles and the like for her publication, *The Bridal Call*, and busied herself with matters concerning the Angelus Temple. It was in Australia that she formally declined to use "the healing service". This despite the hopes of her Australian congregations. Indeed, "the healing service", as such, was to play virtually no role in her activities in the future.

In her absence, the Temple was completed and formally dedicated in 1923. It was not exactly a church for the evangelist saw it as a place where individuals would find salvation and then carry "the good news" elsewhere. The Temple was supposedly dedicated to inter-denominationalism but it became, in fact, the principle edifice of the Church of the Four Square Gospel. It was a handsome building, its interior quite lavishly appointed, and it owed much to the theatre in general. Visitors were to marvel at this new Temple of Solomon. The auditorium seated over 5000, and it was generally filled with worshippers when services were held.

Minnie Kennedy arranged that all regular members of the Temple were slotted into various activities. There was to be a prayer tower where adherents in shifts of two hours duration were actively involved with prayer, not just for themselves but for others whose requests came via the telephone. The Temple switchboard operated on a twenty-four hour basis. There were also to be welfare agencies and other similar social services staffed by the converted.

These activities were all minor in comparison to the star attraction herself. She fully recognised that what she had to produce was a sort of sacred drama, which was to make her even more famous. She used live animals, trained acrobats and hired costumes from the film studios. She had orchestras of almost symphonic size, brass bands and choral groups. Like the Salvation Army, she did not believe that Satan should have all the best tunes. These early dramatic sermons were simplicity itself in comparison to the truly theatrical performances of the 1930s and 1940s. Very astutely, when preaching she continued to wear the simple white dress, the military cloak and the plain shoes. Her appearance ensured a look of spiritual simplicity. To all observers she embodied the pure in heart. Truly she was "Sister Aimée".

In order that her message should have a wider audience, the radio station KFSG (Kall Four Square Gospel) was established. She had used the radio previously on a somewhat casual basis when raising funds to build the Temple, but now there was a regular service called "The Sunshine Hour". It has been estimated that some 200,000 radios were able to receive her sermons. She used KFSG for special causes as well, following the Santa Barbara earthquake in 1925, when she appealed for supplies to assist the afflicted. Her call for help brought instant results: truckloads of food, clothing and blankets appeared as if by magic. Even film stars like Mary Pickford did not get more attention or popular approval than Sister Aimée. She was idolised, loved and adored, but sadly she had few friends and her chief intimates were her mother and her children. Her enemies, disenchanted with her success, sought to find scandal. Her close association with Kenneth Gladstone Ormiston, who had organised KFSG on her behalf, seemed to provide a possible opportunity. Much to their chagrin, he left the radio station and departed from Los Angeles.

She, herself, and her family embarked on a European tour at about the same time. She had a sojourn in France, went on to the Holy Land and made side trips to Italy and Egypt. En route back to the United States, she preached a sermon in London to a vast audience in the Albert Hall. It is interesting to wonder if she had fond recollections of her appearances in the same venue some twenty years earlier. Arriving in Los Angeles in the late spring of 1926, she was given a tremendous welcome by the mayor and a crowd of over ten thousand persons.

She was to regale the public via the radio of her experiences abroad.

About a month after her return, there occurred an event which was to change her life and her image. Accompanied by a friend, she went to the beach which she did not infrequently. Initially, her time was occupied with reading, but then she decided to go for a bathe. She was a strong swimmer and often swam quite far from the shore. When she failed to return after an hour had elapsed, her friend summoned a lifeguard, but there was no sign of the swimmer. Evidently she had drowned. When the news reached the public there was outburst of grief. On 20 June 1926, there was a twelve-hour memorial service with some 6000 inside the Temple and probably twice that number outside. The vacant chair of the evangelist was symbolic.

Three days after this event, she reappeared claiming to have been kidnapped. She said she had managed to escape from her captors and thus regained her freedom. The reporters after interviewing her were sceptical, being convinced that the whole thing was a fraud as her story seemed so improbable. However, if it really had been a fake surely she would have concocted an account that was more credible. When she returned to Los Angeles, she was received with tumultuous cheers from the local populace. Nobody in living memory in the city could recollect such a reception.

Her enemies managed to persuade the local authorities to convene a grand jury to ascertain if a crime of any sort had been committed. Aimée Semple Macpherson and her mother were ordered to appear; the former despite the advice of the latter agreed to testify. Her story of the kidnapping was attacked and derided, reports of an illicit love tryst were leaked to the press and charges of perjury laid. The whole farrago was nonsensical, witnesses were suborned and found to be liars, and the case was dropped. If she had been famous before "the kidnapping" and the trial, she now became world famous, perhaps even notorious.

To vindicate herself, she proposed another tour with the theme, "the story of my life". She was generally received genially and affectionately. In New York she visited Texas Guinan at a nightclub and gave a little sermon which won the applause of the revellers. She charmed some of New York's intellectual elite too. "The Big Apple" decided she was a real star. She had preached in twenty-two cities by the time she returned to Los Angeles. The faithful in the Temple regarded their princess with adoration, affection and acclaim. However, her general appearance had changed: gone was the simple white dress and military cape, replaced by stylish clothes, bobbed hair that was immaculately coiffed, the whole being one of chic elegance. This new look was not to be disadvantageous. Princesses were expected to be glamorous, and as such Sister Aimée was to be no exception.

For the next few years life at the Angelus Temple was fraught with conflict. Minnie Kennedy ceased to be the business manager and retired. Her replacements were either incompetent or dishonest. The general financial situation was such that, despite the generous contributions from the faithful, there was a real shortage of money. Throughout this time the evangelist herself seemed to be amazingly oblivious to the financial crises.

While Minnie Kennedy had no official function in the life at the Temple, she continued to have amiable enough personal contact with her daughter. This was to change in 1930 when there was to be a complete severance of their relationship. A few months later Aimée Semple Macpherson had a complete breakdown. She was to play no public role for nearly a year. To assist in her recovery, she and her daughter went on a lengthy cruise, and when she returned she was given the usual rapturous welcome by the local people.

Almost at once she was to be at her creative best. Her sermons now were not only verbal productions, but were part of a great theatrical performance. Every gesture was stylised, the costumes worn by the choirs and herself were selected with infinite care, the musicians were increasingly professional and the whole mise-en-scène could not have been bettered by any film producer.

Yet despite the acclaim, her life was empty. The breach with her mother left her lonely, her children had their own lives and she was on her own. To alleviate this state of state of affairs she sought companionship with a rather dreary and very overweight opera singer who had starred in her oratorio, *The Iron Furnace*. David Hutton, despite his somewhat egregious appearance – he was once described as being rather like a muffin with eyes – had a curious sexual magnetism which women found attractive and Aimée Semple Macpherson was no exception.

Following their marriage, the bridal couple made a tour of evangelising and preaching. En route they called at San Quentin prison. Ironically, two of its denizens had played not insignificant roles in the life of Aimée Semple Macpherson. One, Asa Keynes, who had been the chief prosecutor in the trial of 1926, was imprisoned for accepting bribes; the other, Cromwell Ormsby, a sometime corrupt and incompetent business manager for the Angelus Temple, had been gaoled for jury tampering. The evangelist and her spouse proceeded to offer prayers that the two convicts might be led to a better life.

California was beginning to experience the worst aspects of "the Great Depression". Aimée Semple Macpherson organised a major charitable assistance programme. Nobody, regardless of religious, political or ethnic background, was turned away. A soup kitchen was established under the management of her husband, and it was said that in one month some 80,000 people received food. For all of these efforts, and she did not lessen her role as the church director, she gained the respect and the true regard of the city of Los Angeles, in particular from its more conservative denizens.

The mid-1930s found her as active as ever, preaching in many American and Canadian cities, visiting Japan and India as well. Much of this frenetic activity was a way of escaping from reality. Her marriage had failed, the affairs of the Temple were muddled, while conflicts with her colleagues and her daughter, Roberta Semple, increased the tensions. A series of highly publicised lawsuits did not improve the situations. In an attempt to extricate herself from her difficulties, she selected Giles Knight to manage her affairs. For seven years he was to be in charge with good results.

With the outbreak of war in 1941, she involved herself in various patriotic activities. The United States Army made her an honorary colonel and various government departments gave her citations. Even the press saluted her as a national icon. The ageing prima donna of the pulpit managed to convince the outside world that she was unchanged, still the dazzling and charismatic individual. She looked handsome and was always elegant, but physically she was very frail.

The Knight regime ended in the spring of 1944. The parting was amiable, unlike the leave-taking of Minnie Kennedy or Roberta Semple. Knight was replaced by Rolf Macpherson. In a sense Aimée Semple Macpherson believed she was re-creating the happy times of some two decades earlier. Somehow the new state of affairs with Rolf at the helm seems to have restored her self-confidence. She made plans for another tour and for a bigger and better production at the Temple.

On 25 September 1944 she and Rolf and an entourage arrived in Oakland, California, where she was to dedicate a new tabernacle and to deliver her now-famous discourse, "The Story of my Life". She did not retire early. Her son bade her goodnight about eleven o'clock. What exactly happened after that time is not precisely known. She seems to have taken some extra-strength sedatives, the next morning Rolf Macpherson found her in a coma and she died on 27 September 1944. She was 53 years of age. Her death was adjudged to have been the result of an accident, as it indeed it certainly was.

She was never suicidal even in the darkest times of her life. The barbiturates taken in a considerable dosage, combined with her general poor health, ensured that she could not survive.

If the return from the kidnap incident in 1926 had been greeted with warmth and enthusiasm by her followers, so the arrival of the corpse was once again the occasion for a vast demonstration. This time it was not to the tune "California here I come", as previously, but to more sombre and melancholy music.

The body lay in state, the coffin was open and she was seen in her simple white dress and her blue military cape. This was the way most members of the Temple preferred to remember her. It has been estimated that over 50,000 people came to pay their last respects.

The funeral was, of course, spectacular. There were 2000 mourners in the Temple in the company of 1700 ministers, all of whom had been personally ordained by the deceased. It was the final and perhaps the most sumptuous theatrical production with which she would be associated. Her former husband, Harold Macpherson, was present, as was her mother, Minnie Kennedy. Her daughter, Roberta Semple, was unable to reach Los Angeles because of war-time travel restrictions. Rolf Macpherson and his family were the chief mourners. She was buried in Forest Lawn Cemetery on her birthday, a fitting occasion for one so addicted to special events.

It is not easy to evaluate Aimée Semple Macpherson. Her enemies, and there were many, saw her as a sham and a fraud milking the innocent and credulous of funds to finance her own extravagant existence. Those who were her parishioners regarded her as a veritable saint, pure and holy and almost without sin. Yet, she who had swum against the tide was for her day the most influential female evangelist, perhaps even today the most famous and certainly the most notorious. She brought the Christian message to the widest of congregations. She left a legacy that few other religious revivalists could emulate. The Four Square Gospel Church survived her, a denomination that reckons its membership as being over a million. The Angelus Temple is still a place of pilgrimage and worship, and legions of tourists have visited it over the years as a major attraction in Los Angeles. For a girl dedicated by her mother to God, it could be said without too much of a contradiction that she had fulfilled her destiny.

SELECTED BIBLIOGRAPHY

Aegerter, Emmanuel, *Madame Guyon*, 1941.
Andrews, E., *People called Shakers, a Search for the perfect Society*, 1944.
Austin, Alfred, *Aimee Semple Macpherson*, 1980.
Bahr, Robert, *Heart of All Saints, the Story of Aimee Semple Macpherson*, 1979.
Baldwin, Monica, *I Leap Over the Wall*, 1949.
Brown, Frances, *Joanna Southcott: The Woman Clothed with the Sun*, 2002.
Bruneau, Marie, *Women Mystics Confront the Modern World*, 1998.
Caldwell, Daniel, *Esoteric World of Madame Blavatsky*, 1999.
Cather, Willa and Georgina Milmine, *The Life of Mary Baker Eddy and the History of Christian Science*, Rev. ed., 1990.
Cranston, Sylvia, *The Extraordinary Life of Madame Blavatsky*, 1993.
Dubay, Thomas, *The Fire Within. Saint Teresa, St John of the Cross and the Gospel of Prayer*, 1990.
Eddy, Mary Baker, *Science and Health*, 1902.
Francis, Richard, *Ann Lee*, 2001.
Glynn, Joseph, *Eternal Mystics*, 1982.
Gaspard-Huit, Pierre, *L'Illuminatrice Helena Blavatsky*, 1995.
Guyon, Mme. *Autobiography*, Translated T.T. Allen, 1897.
Harris, E.B. Ward: *A Nun Goes to the Dogs: A Biography of Mother Cecilia Mary*. 1969.
Hopkins, James K., *Woman to Deliver her People, Joanna Southcott and English Millenarianism*, 1982.
Johnson, Jan, *Madame Guyon, Woman of Faith*, 1990.
Knapton, Ernest John, *Our Lady of the Holy Alliance, the Life of Julia de Krudener*, 1939.
Knox, Ronald, *Enthusiasm: A Chapter in the History of Religion*, 1954.
Ley, Francis, *Madame de Krudener et son temps 1764-1824*, 1962.
Maclean, John P., *A Bibliography of Shaker Literature with an Introductory Study*, 1971.
Mayer, Donald P., *The Positive Thinker*, 2000.
Moore, Katherine, *She For God*, 1955.
Neame, Alan, *The Holy Maid of Kent, the Life of Elizabeth Barton*, 1971.
Papasogli, Giorgio, *St Teresa of Avila*, n.d.
Powell, Lymon P., *Mary Baker Eddy, A Life Size Portrait*, 1991.
Royal, Samuel J., *A Biographical Dictionary of Eighteenth-Century Methodism*, 1997.
Slone, Carol, *St Teresa of Avila, Author of a Heroic Life*, 1995.
Stein, S., *The Shaker Experience in America: A History of the United Society of Believers*, 1992.
Swark, Scott T. and Bill Finney, *Shaker Life, Art and Architecture, Hands to Work, Hearts to God*, 1999.
Teresa of Avila, *The collected Works of St Teresa of Avila*, Rev. ed., 1940.
Upham, T. C., *Life of Madame Guyon*, 2000.
Washington, Peter, *Madame Blavatski's Baboon*, 1996.

Index

Abbeymere, St Dunstan's, 104-5, 107
Adelaide, Queen, 99, 101
Adyar, 137-9, 141
Aksakov, Alexander, 132
Alcott, Bronson, 115
Alexander I, Tsar, 84, 88-94
Antonio, brother of Teresa, 26
Arnaud, Angélique, 8
Arnauld, 37
Ascot Priory, 107, 108
Ashby-de-la-Zouch, 50, 57
Askew, Anne, 8
Astor, Lady, 122
Audley, Sir Thomas, 21
Augustine, St., 7
Avila, Convent of the Incarnation, 25-6, 28-9, 31-2, 34-5

Babula, 135-6
Baden, 86-7, 91; Grand Duke of, 86
Bagration, Princess, 129
Baker, Albert, 111
Baker, Ebenezer (Benny) Foster, 119-21
Baker, Mary Morse – see Mary Baker Eddy
Baker, Noah and Abigail, 111
Bangor, Bishop of, 21
Barlow, Anne, 51
Barry, George, 116
Barton, Elizabeth, 11-23
Bartrop, Mabel, 79
Bastille, 43-4, 83
Beas, convent at, 32-3
Benedict, St., 97
Benson, Joseph, 54
Berkheim, Charles Baron, 88, 93
Bernini, 35
Besant, Annie, 8, 139-41
Betanelly, Michael Constantinovitch, 132-3
Bey, Master Serapis, 133-4
Bingley, Sarah, 115
Birmingham, 145-6, 148
Blau, Madame, 85
Blavatsky, Helena Petrovna (Madam Blavatsky), 73, 118, 125-141
Blavatsky, Nikifor Vassilievich, 127-8, 130
Blessington, Marguerite, 112
Bocking, Edward, 11-4, 17, 20-2
Boleyn, Anne, 15-6, 18-9, 23
Bolingbroke, Lord, 50-1
Bonner, Edmund, 16
Booth, Catherine, 8
Booth, William, 8
Bossuet, Bishop Jacques, 43-4
Boston, 117-9, 121
Boucher, Joan, 8
Bourgogne, Duc de, 42-3
Bourignon, Antoinette, 8
Bridget of Sweden, St., 7
Bronte, Charlotte, 126
Buckingham, Duke of,19
Buckingham, Lady,50
Butler, Sir James,122
Butterfield, William, 104

Cairo, 129, 131
Cambridge, 53, 57
Cambridge, Mass., 122
Campbell, Diana, 105
Campbell, Lord, 103
Canterbury, 11, 13-6, 18-9, 21
Cardinal Pacelli, 151, 152
Castlereagh, Lord, 90
Cather, Willa, 121
Catherine of Aragon, 14, 16, 18, 21, 23
Catherine of Siena, St., 7, 35
Catherine II, 125
Catherine, Mother Eldress, 108
Chadwick, Owen, 109
Chambers, Catherine, 99
Chambers, John, 97, 99
Chandler, William, 121
Charles I of England, 38
Charles V, Holy Roman Emperor, 15, 17
Chavchavadzes, 127
Chicago, 119, 160-1
Chittendon, 132-3

Clark, Henrietta, 119
Clement VII, 15, 18-20
Cobb, Thomas, 11-2, 14
Cofts, Hiram, 115
Colles, William, 104
Collins, Mabel, 138
Concord, N.H., 118, 120-1
Constant, Benjamin, 90
Constantinople, 128-9
Cooksley, W. G., 105
Coulomb, Alexis, 136
Coulomb, Emma, 131, 136-8
Court-at-Street, 13-4, 18, 20
Courtenay family, 18-9
Cranmer, Thomas, 17, 20
Crashaw, Richard, 25
Crawford, Francis Marian, 137
Cromwell, Thomas, 18-21,
Crosly, Sarah, 8
Cutting, Emma – see Emma Coulomb

d'Avila, Father Juan, 30, 32, 35
Davio, Silvestre, 18-20
Davis, Andrew Jackson, 132
de Cetina, Father Diego, 27
de Krudener, Juliana, 81-94
de la Bedoyere, General, 90
de la Mothe, Abbé, 42
de la Mothe, Claude Bouvières, 37-8
de la Mothe, Jeanne Marie Bouvières - see Jeanne Marie Guyon
de Noailles, Bishop of Chalons, 43
de Poncier, Archbishop Adam, 149-1
de Roo, Bishop Remi, 153-6
de St Pierre, Bernardin, 83
de Stael, Madame, 84, 90
Deving, Richard, 20
Devonport, 98-9, 106, 109
Dimsdale, Baron, 81
Dodd, Ethel Cecilia, 143-157
Dodd, John and Lillian, 143-50
Don Alonso, 25, 26, 27
Donnington Park, 48-50, 53
Doubleday, General Abner, 134
Duke, Archbishop William, 151-2

Earl of Moira, 51
Eddy brothers, 132, 133
Eddy, Asa Gilbert, 116-8
Eddy, Mary Baker, 111-22
Edison, Thomas, 134
Edwin, Catherine, 51

Elizabeth of Tottenham, 17
Elizabeth, Tsarina of Russia, 88
Emma of Hawaii, Queen, 107
Empaytaz, Henri, 87-91
Erskine, Lady Anne, 57
Exeter, Bishop of, 73
Exeter, Lady, 19, 21
Exeter, Marquess of, 18, 21, 23

Fadeyev, Helena Andreyevna – see Hahn, Helena Andreyevna von
Fadeyevs, 126-8, 130
Fénelon, Archbishop of Cambrai, 37, 42-4
Fisher, Bishop John, 16, 18-9, 21-2
Fletcher, William, 54-5
Fontaines, Frederick, 86-7
Four Square Gospel, Church of the, 165, 171
Fox sisters, 8, 113
Francis de Sales, St., 98
Francis of Assisi, St., 27
Franco, General, 35
Frederick of Prussia, 86
Frederick, Prince of Wales, 51
Frye, Calvin, 119

Galitzine, Prince Alexander, 127-8
Galitzine, Prince, 89, 93-4
Galitzine, Princess, 93
Gardiner, Bishop Stephen, 16
Garibaldi, 131
Glover, George Washington, 112, 113, 118, 121
Glover, George, 112
Glover, Mary – see Mary Baker Eddy
Gold, Henry, 18, 20
Gold, Thomas, 20
Good Shepherd Animal Shelter, 153-6
Goodman, Margaret, 106
Gorham Judgment, 103
Gracian, Jeronian, 32-5
Greenfield, Ann, 51
Grenfell, Joyce, 122
Guyon (daughter), 40
Guyon (third son), 39
Guyon, Armand Jacques, 39-40
Guyon, Jacques, 38-40
Guyon, Jeanne Marie, 37-44, 86
Guyon, Mme (mother-in-law), 39

Hadleigh, Thomas, 20
Hahn, Helena Andreyevna von, 125-6
Hahn, Helena Petrovna von - see Helena

Petrovna Blavatsky
Hahn, Nicholas Gustavitch von, 131
Hahn, Peter Alexyevitch von, 125-6, 128, 132
Hahn, Vera Petrovna von, 130
Hannon, Judge Septimus, 119
Hargott – see Fontaines, Frederick
Harlow, Calvin, 65
Harrison, Vernon, 138
Hastings, Elizabeth, 48
Hastings, Francis, 48
Hastings, Lady Betty, 49
Hastings, Lady Margaret, 49
Hastings, Theophilus, 48
Hatchard, John, 101, 102, 105
Hawker, Robert Stephen, 102
Henderson, Major, 136
Henrietta Maria, 38
Henry I of England, 14
Henry VIII, 11, 13-23
Hill, Bishop James, 152-3
Hocknall, John, 63-4, 66
Hodgson, Richard, 137-8, 140
Home, Daniel Douglas, 134
Home, Daniel, 129
Honolulu, Bishop of, 107
Hopkins, Nicholas, 19
Hughes, Marian Rebecca, 97
Hume, Alan, 136
Hume, David, 51
Hutchinson, Anne, 8
Hutton, David, 168

Ignatius, Brother, 107
Ingersoll, 160-1
Ingham, Benjamin, 49
Ireland, Shadrack, 67

Jeffries, Augusta, 126
Jesuits, 105
John Chrysostom, St., 7
John of the Cross, St., 7, 27, 30, 32-3, 35
John the Baptist, St., 62
Johnson, Doctor Samuel, 7, 50
Juan de la Miseria, 30
Judge, William, 133, 139-40
Jung-Stilling, Henrick, 86

Keber, Father, 153-4
Kellner, Pastor, 93
Kennedy, Aimeé Elizabeth —see Aimeé Semple Macpherson
Kennedy, James, 159

Kennedy, Minnie, 159, 161-170
Kennedy, Richard, 115
Kent, William, 48
Keynes, Asa, 169
King Milan Obrenevitch, 130
Kingsford, Anna, 137, 139
Kissilev, Countess, 129
Kitchener, Ontario, 162
Knight, Giles, 169
Koot Hoomi, mahatma, 136
Kosse, 81, 82, 87, 92, 93
Krishnamurti, Jiddu, 9, 141
Krudener, Burchard von, 82-4
Krudener, Juliette von, 83-4, 88, 93
Krudener, Paul von, 91
Krudener, Sophie von, 83-4, 88
Kulavein, Anna, 126
Kummer, Marie, 86

La Combe, Father François, 39-2, 44
Landon, Laetitia Elizabeth, 112
Langton, Emma, 97-8
Latimer, Bishop Hugh, 20
Law, William, 50
Leadbetter, Charles, 138-9, 141
Lee, Ann, 61-69
Lee, William, 64, 66, 68
Leeds, 107
Linacre, Thomas, 11
Lisbon, 35
Lisle, Lord, 22
Liverpool, 63
London, 21-2, 52-3, 61, 75, 78, 97, 107, 127, 129, 135, 137-8, 143-4, 160, 162, 167
Los Angeles, 162, 164, 166-71; Angelus Temple, 162, 165-71
Lothian, Lord, 122
Louis XIV, 8, 38, 42-4, 84
Louise of Prussia, Queen, 85
Lourdes Castle, 41
Loyola's *Spiritual Exercises*, 27
Lucca, Duke of, 129
Luther, Martin, 16

M, mahatma, 136
Macaulay, Lord, 74
Macpherson, Aimeé Semple, 159-171
Macpherson, Harold Stuart ("Mack"), 161-3, 170
Macpherson, Rolf, 161, 165, 169-70
Madras, 136-7

Magnon, Madame, 132
Maintenon, Madame de, 42-3
Manchester, 66, 69
Margaret of Scotland, St., 157
Marie de l'Incarnation, Sister, 40
Martin, Father Claude, 40
Mary Julia, Sister, 156
Mary Louise, Sister, 151
Mary Magdalene, St., 18
Mary Tudor (Mary I), 11, 14, 17-9, 23, 78, 97
Mary Ursula, Sister, 153
Masters, Richard, 11-2, 20
Maud, Empress, 14
Maximilla, 7
Mazzini, Giuseppe, 131
Meacham, Joseph, 65, 69
Medina del Campo, St Joseph's, 30, 32, 34
Metropolitan Philaret, 89
Metrovich, Agardi, 129-31
Metrovich, Yuri, 130
Molinos, Miguel de, 41
Montague, Lord, 18-9, 23
Montaubon, Duchesse de, 37
More, Thomas, 13, 17, 19, 21-2
Moscheles, Ignaz, 127
Mother Ann - see Lee, Ann
Mother Cecilia - see Ethel Cecilia Dodd
Mother Gertrude Clare, 149
Mother Millicent Mary, 146, 149
Muller, Adam, 85-6
Munchausen, Baron, 131

Napoleon, 85, 89-90
Neel, Alexandra David, 9
New York, 63-4, 68, 131-3, 136, 161, 168
Ney, Marshal, 90
Nicholas I, Tsar, 125
Nicholas II, Tsar, 127
Nightingale, Florence, 103, 106, 143, 150, 157, 164
Niskeyuna, 64-5, 67-9
Noyes, Rufus King, 117

Ochondo, Marquis, 88
Olcott, Henry Steel, 132-1
Ormiston, Kenneth Gladstone, 166
Ormsby, Cromwell, 169
Oxford, 53, 102

Paine, Thomas, 77
Paris, 35, 38, 40-1, 43, 82-4, 91, 131, 140

Parrington, John, 64
Paschkov, Lydia, 131
Patterson, Daniel, 113-4
Patterson, Mary – see Mary Baker Eddy
Paul, Grand Duke, 83
Paul, St., 7
Peter the Great, 125
Philip II of Spain, 30
Phillpotts, Henry, Bishop of Exeter, 98-1, 103-5
Pickford, Mary, 166
Pitt the Elder, William, 56
Pope Pius XII – see Cardinal Pacelli
Portland, Maine, 114
Eboli, Prince and Princess of, 30-1
Providence, R.I., 161-3
Prynne, George, 105
Pusey, Edward Bouverie, 7, 97, 100, 102, 106-8
Pushkin, 125

Quimby, Phineas, 113-5

Rasputin, 130
Rathbone, Valentine, 67
Récamier, Madame, 90
Rich, Rev. Hugh, 18-20
Riga, 81-4, 87, 92-3
Rodrigo, brother of Teresa, 25
Roley, Richard, 20
Rousseau, Jean Jacques, 81, 83
Rowson, Alfred Lawson, 129
Rugdevo, 130

Salisbury, Countess of, 23
San Francisco, 107
San Quentin prison, 169
Sanborn, Mabola, 112
Sanbornton, 112
Santa Barbara, 166
Saxe-Weimar, Grand Duchess of, 92
Schumann, Clara, 127
Selina, Lady Huntingdon, 47-58
Sellon, Anna, 97
Sellon, Commander Richard, 97-9
Sellon, Lydia, 97-109
Sellon, William, 97
Semple, Robert, 160-1
Semple, Roberta Starr, 161, 169-0
Seymour, Hobart, 105
Shaw, George Bernard, 140
Shirley, Anne (née Elliott), 48

Shirley, Elizabeth, 48
Shirley, Lady Selina - see Selina, Lady Huntingdon
Shirley, Laurence, 47
Shirley, Mary, 48
Shirley, Walter, 47
Shirley, Washington, Earl Ferrers, 47-8
Shrine, Elizabeth, 51
Singh, Prince Dulep, 129
Sinnett, Alfred, 135-6, 138
Sisters of Mercy, Devonport, 99-101, 103, 106, 108
Sisters of the Holy Cross, 97, 99, 100, 102, 106
Smith, John, 78
Society of the Incarnation of the Eternal Son, 147-9
Society of the Love of Jesus, 150, 152-4
Society of the Precious Blood, 146-7, 149
Southcott, Joanna, 9, 71-79
Southcott, Shiloh, 77-8
Southey, Robert, 73
Spofford, Daniel, 116
Spurrell, James, 104-5
St Anthony's College, 151
St Anthony's House, 150
St Cyr, academy of, 42-3
St Petersburg, 81, 89, 92-4, 128
St Mary's Priory, Victoria, 152-6
Standerin, Abraham, 61, 63-4
Stead, W. T., 140
Stockholm, 81
Stroudza, Roxana, 88-9, 92
Stuckey family, 79
Syon Abbey, 18-9, 23

Tallinen, 81
Teresa of Avila, 7, 25-35
Terrot, Ann, 99
Thwaites, Edward, 13
Thwaites, Henry, 20
Tibet, 9
Tiflis 127-8, 130
Toledo, 25, 28, 31
Tonbridge, chapel, 52
Townley, Jane, 75
Tractarians, 101, 105
Trefuca House, 53, 56
Trefuca Isaf, 53
Tunstall, Cuthbert, 16

Turnbull, Sister (and Mother) Bertha, 108, 109
Twain, Mark, 120
Tyburn, 19, 22
Tyndale, William, 8, 14, 16

Ulrike, Anna, 81
Underwood, Ann, 75
Ursulines, 98

Valladolid, 35
Van Rensalaer estate, 64
Vancouver, 149-52
Vaugiraud, 43
Venice, 82-4
Vestris, Madame, 82
Victoria, Queen, 129, 143
Vietinghof, Juliana von – see Juliana de Krudener
Vietinghof, Otto Herman, Baron von, 81
Vietinghofs, von, 81-2

Wachmeister, Constance, 138
Wardley, James and Jane, 61, 62, 63
Warham, Archbishop, 11-5, 17
Washington, George, 56
Waterloo, Battle of, 90
Wentworth, Anne, 13-4
Wesley, Charles, 49-50, 54
Wesley, John, 8, 49-50, 54, 57
Wesley, Patty, 8
Whitfield, George, 49-51, 52, 54-7
Whittaker, James, 63-4, 66, 68
Wiggin, James Harvey, 118
Wilder, Alexander, 134
Wilkinson, Jemima, 8
Winnifrede, Sister – see Augusta Wolfe
Witte, Catherine, 127
Witte, Sergius, 127-8, 130, 141
Witte, Yuli, 127
Wittgenstein, Prince, 140
Wolfe, Augusta, 104
Wolkonsky, Prince, 89
Wolsey, Cardinal Thomas, 14-8
Wordsworth, William, 101
Wright, Lucy, 69
Wright, Wallace, 115

Yeats, William Butler, 73, 139
Yermolova, Madame, 128
Zinzendorf, Count Nicholas, 85